closer to GOD

for newcomers

meet the Real Jesus

40 GUIDED BIBLE READINGS

Belinda Pollard

Scripture Union, 207–2009 Queensway, Bletchley, Milton Keynes, MK2 2EB, England
Email: info@scriptureunion.org.uk
Website: www.scriptureunion.org.uk

Scripture Union Australia
Locked Bag 2, Central Coast Business Centre, NSW 2252
Website: www.su.org.au

Scripture Union USA
P.O. Box 987, Valley Forge, PA 19482
Website: www.scriptureunion.org.

Printed and bound in Great Britain by Creative Print and Design (Wales) Ebbw Vale.

Designed by Scratch the Sky (Design@scratchthesky.com).

Scripture Union is an international Christian charity working with churches in more than 130 countries, providing resources to bring the good news about Jesus Christ to children, young people and families and to encourage them to develop spiritually through the Bible and prayer.

As well as our network of volunteers, staff and associates who run holidays, church-based events and school Christian groups, we produce a wide range of publications and support those who use our resources through training programmes.

For enquiries about the work of Soul Survivor, contact:

Soul Survivor, Unit 2, Paramount Industrial Estate, Sandown Road, Watford, WD24 7XF
Telephone: 0870 0543331
Email: info@soulsurvivor.com
Website: www.soulsurvivor.com/uk

contents...

foreword

Dear friends,

I'm very pleased that you've got this book in your hands. It means you are either wanting to think about Jesus and figure out who he is, or you've discovered him and want to know more. This is a guide to help you get into the most exciting book in the world, the Bible – a book that will allow you to find out more about God, his church and his love for you.

These guided readings lay out some of the basics of what a Christian believes and how you can grow through a relationship with Jesus, allowing you to discover important truths for yourself. This is a wonderful tool, to help dig deep into the treasure chest God's given you in the Bible.

If you are beginning your search for Jesus, you'll find this a helpful way in: to see what the Bible says about him; unpacking his words, giving them some context and making them easier to understand.

If you're a new Christian, I am thrilled to welcome you to the family. There's so much to know and so far to grow – it can be both really exciting and really frustrating! There are two main things to remember. One, spend time with Jesus: praying (speaking to God), reading the Bible and worshipping him (singing along to a worship CD might help). Two, get involved in a church. God wants you to be in community with other believers – it will be one of the main things to help you grow in your faith.

Thank you so much for being a part of SOULINTHECITY. This summer, over 600 churches across London and some 15,000 young people from around the world took part in a massive effort to share the good news of Jesus with as many people from as many ways of life as possible. We are so excited for you, are behind you and are praying for you!

Love

Mike Pilavachi
Director, SOULINTHECITY

So who is this man?

This is a book about Jesus Christ. Twenty-one centuries after he walked the dusty roads of Palestine, he is still famous. Our dating system pivots around the year of his birth. Every day around the globe, people quote and misquote him, use his name as a swear word and argue about his significance.

This book is designed to help you delve into the Bible for yourself. It will help you find out what difference Jesus can make in your daily life. It will help you discover what it means to belong to God and become part of his worldwide family. Over the next forty days, we will read selections from two books of the Bible: a biography of Jesus and a short history of his first followers. These are living, breathing accounts, full of conflict and compassion, great courage and narrow escapes, and a hope that emerges from the midst of tragedy. A man named Luke compiled them from eyewitness accounts and was even present at some of the events. The purpose of reading these passages is not just so that you can know more *about* Jesus, but so that you can truly *know* him. Meet Jesus Christ: poor carpenter's son, friend to the unlovable, Son of God, your Saviour.

And who is this woman?

Belinda Pollard writes for Scripture Union's Bible guide, *Closer to God*. She lives in Brisbane, Australia and works as a freelance journalist and editor. She says, 'I have been motivated to write this book by a passion for reaching out to people who are looking for purpose in life, love that doesn't wear out and a sense of belonging, because I believe Jesus is the only person who can give them those things.'

What's so special about the Bible?

The Bible is central to the Christian faith because it is a book about Jesus Christ. The letters on the page are not somehow magical, but God's Holy Spirit speaks to his people through the message of this book. Even though it was written thousands of years ago, the Bible is not a 'dead' book, but a living message from God to you. Daily life has changed dramatically over that period of time, but human nature hasn't changed and God's nature hasn't changed. God has something to say to you that is relevant to everything you will ever face in your life.

What's in it?

The Bible is not strictly just one book, but a whole library of sixty-six books by a variety of authors, written between about 2000 BC and AD 100. The first thirty-nine books, Genesis to Malachi, make up the Old Testament. It contains history, poetry and prophecy, telling the story of God's relationship with the Jewish people and pointing forward to the coming of Jesus Christ. The other twenty-seven books in the New Testament were written after Jesus came. They contain four different biographies of Jesus, a history of the beginnings of the Christian church and correspondence from early Christian leaders about important issues of faith.

Despite this diversity, it hangs together as one book – God's Word.

How do I use it?

As the Bible is such a special book, we can't pick and choose which bits we're going to accept and which to ignore. All of it is God's message, and it is just waiting for us to pick it up and read it. However, we will understand it even better when we know the culture of a given period and the purpose of the writing. For example, when the Bible says, 'In the heavens he has pitched a tent for the sun, which is like a bridegroom coming forth from his pavilion' (Psalm 19:4,5), it is being poetic about the power of God, not making a scientific statement about the nature of the sun. Archeologists, literary scholars and theologians have spent countless hours poring over the Bible and they have made their findings freely available. *Closer to God* is one easy way to access some of their knowledge.

You will see numbers marked in the Bible readings reproduced in this book. The larger number is the chapter and the smaller numbers throughout the text are verses. They are referred to like this: Luke 1:10, where the book is called Luke, the chapter is number 1 and the verse is 10.

Can I trust it?

Scholars who study ancient texts say that, the more copies you have of a text and the older they are, the more certain you can be that what you are reading is what was originally written. There are enormous numbers of ancient copies of the Bible text. There are only very minor variations between all the copies, and none of the differences threaten any major point of Christian doctrine. It is the most trustworthy ancient document available in the modern world.

What the Bible says about itself...

All Scripture is God-breathed and is useful for teaching, rebuking, correcting and training in righteousness, so that the man of God may be thoroughly equipped for every good work. (2 Timothy 3:16,17)

Above all, you must understand that no prophecy of Scripture came about by the prophet's own interpretation. For prophecy never had its origin in the will of man, but men spoke from God as they were carried along by the Holy Spirit. (2 Peter 1:20,21)

For the word of God is living and active. Sharper than any double-edged sword, it penetrates even to dividing soul and spirit, joints and marrow; it judges the thoughts and attitudes of the heart. (Hebrews 4:12)

Prayer: Conversation with God

Relationships are about communication. Prayer is how humans communicate with God. There are all kinds of prayers in the Bible: of pleading, fear, anger, passion, adoration.

Prayer doesn't need special words or formulas. Just talk to God the way you normally talk. He loves to hear from you. Tell him what you think of him, what is going on around you, ask him to take some action in your life or the lives of others, or just enjoy his presence. Nothing is too big or too small for God – you can pray for world peace or a school exam. Pray with respect because God is the Lord of the universe, but also pray with trust and confidence, because he is your Father. You can be confident that he will listen to you.

You can pray with a group or alone. You can pray out loud or silently inside your head. When you become a Christian, God's Holy Spirit actually lives inside you, so you can talk to God at any time and he will hear you. Sometimes you won't be able to find the words, and then God steps in: 'the Spirit himself intercedes for us with groans that words cannot express' (Romans 8:26).

Prayer is a two-way conversation. People might say 'God told me…' This doesn't usually mean they heard an audible voice, although sometimes they will have. Often it means that they were aware of God speaking to them about a given situation through something in the Bible. Sometimes after much prayer they are convinced that God wants them to take a certain course of action, as their Bible readings, the advice of godly friends and events in their lives all seem to point in one direction. If someone says they have a message from God for you, test it against what the Bible says, and talk to God and a church leader about it.

This book will give you pointers for the kinds of things you might like to talk to God about. Many Christians have found it refreshing and spiritually nourishing to develop a habit of regularly talking to God. You might find it seems a little awkward at first but, as you get to know God better, it will become more natural, and a very special part of your life.

What is Christianity?

Christianity is not a code of conduct. It is not a social club. It is a loving relationship – with God and with his people. Christians base their beliefs on the Bible, which is the record of God's dealings with his people over thousands of years. It is essentially a book about Jesus Christ, who is the one who made having a loving relationship with God possible.

Where did everything go wrong?

The Bible says that the world was made perfect. Humans enjoyed perfect relationship with God, with each other and with the planet. But then the first humans, who were given the free will to choose, decided that they'd rather control their own lives. They rejected God. The result was that everything was ruined. Every relationship was destroyed. People feared and ignored God. People hated and killed each other. The planet, instead of giving food and enjoyment, gave earthquakes and natural disasters. This was a very, very serious crime. The sentence for it was death. The human race and the planet were put on death row. This broken, messed-up world had to be demolished.

What did God do about it?

The story doesn't end there. God loved the people he'd made so very much that he wanted to rescue them. But he wouldn't be fair and just if he ignored the problem, and the mess wouldn't resolve itself – the death penalty had to be served. That's where Jesus comes in. Jesus was both God and human. He was the only perfect human who had ever lived, so he didn't need to be on death row. And yet he volunteered to take the death sentence so we could get off death row. Because of his perfection, his one death was enough to take the death penalty for every human who ever lived. Everyone. Even Adolf Hitler and Pol Pot.

What about us?

But we have to want it. Not everyone will choose Jesus. Some will prefer it on death row – maybe it's where all their friends are, or they prefer to try to find some other way out. But there is no other way out. The only way out is full pardon, through taking hold of Jesus' death in our place. God yearns for every human to take advantage of his rescue plan, but he won't force us to, because that would be a fundamental violation of relationship. If a man loved me so much that he kidnapped me and made me marry him against my will, I don't think I'd be overly grateful to him or keen to love him back. Love must be voluntary, or it's not love.

If you haven't yet chosen Jesus, but you're fed up with life on death row, and you want to change sides now, it's remarkably simple. You just have to tell God, in simple words. You may like to pray the following prayer, which you can say out loud or in your head:

Dear God, I'm sorry that I've been part of the problem and haven't lived in loving relationship with you. I believe that Jesus is the way out. Please rescue me and change my life now.

If you've prayed this prayer, or one like it, God is overjoyed, and the Bible says that even the angels in heaven are celebrating. You are so precious to God! Jesus' death has cleansed you of everything wrong you have ever done, no matter how major or how trivial. He will keep restoring you from every mistake you might make in the future. The door of your dank, dark cell on death row has swung open. Step into the sunlight and breathe the fresh air of a loving and open relationship with God.

How to use this book...

This book contains 40 separate readings, which you can use as a meditation or devotional every day for nearly six weeks. We will be reading selections from the Gospel of Luke and the Acts of the Apostles. Both were written by a man named Luke, who travelled widely with the apostle Paul, one of the early Christian leaders. If you have a full Bible available, you may find it interesting to read right through both books. There are lots more fascinating stories and insights in them that we simply couldn't squeeze into our little book!

Each day's comments are based on the format of *Closer to God*, produced by Scripture Union four times each year with continually fresh and refreshing insights into God's message to us.

Prepare

Some thoughts designed to help you get your heart and mind ready for what the Holy Spirit wants to say to you.

Read

Each selection is reproduced in full, so that you can easily take this book with you wherever you go. As you read, ask yourself: What's the main point of this passage? What is God showing me about himself or about my life?

Explore

Some comments and explanations, helping you to go more deeply into the passage, and strengthen your understanding of Jesus.

Respond

Some points on how to pray and act in response to what God has told you.

A bonus in this booklet is a quotation box, containing verses from other parts of the Bible that relate to the theme each day.

Great expectations

Prepare *You are about to embark on a wonderful journey into God's message to you, the Bible. Say a short prayer, out loud or silently in your head, asking God to help you understand what he will say to you today and in the coming weeks.*

Read Luke 1:26—38

26 In the sixth month, God sent the angel Gabriel to Nazareth, a town in Galilee, 27 to a virgin pledged to be married to a man named Joseph, a descendant of David. The virgin's name was Mary. 28 The angel went to her and said, "Greetings, you who are highly favoured! The Lord is with you." 29 Mary was greatly troubled at his words and wondered what kind of greeting this might be. 30 But the angel said to her, "Do not be afraid, Mary, you have found favour with God. 31 You will be with child and give birth to a son, and you are to give him the name Jesus. 32 He will be great and will be called the Son of the Most High. The Lord God will give him the throne of his father David, 33 and he will reign over the house of Jacob for ever; his kingdom will never end." 34 "How will this be," Mary asked the angel, "since I am a virgin?" 35 The angel answered, "The Holy Spirit will come upon you, and the power of the Most High will overshadow you. So the holy one to be born will be called the Son of God.

36 Even Elizabeth your relative is going to have a child in her old age, and she who was said to be barren is in her sixth month. 37 For nothing is impossible with God." 38 "I am the Lord's servant," Mary answered. "May it be to me as you have said." Then the angel left her.

Explore Our world abounds with stories of unusual births. Surrogates, single women and grandmothers are having babies. I even knew a woman who, like Mary's elderly cousin Elizabeth (v 36), was declared infertile by her doctors, only to become suddenly and astonishingly pregnant some years later.

However, only one child in the history of the planet was ever conceived without any contribution from a human father. His name is Jesus (which means 'God is salvation'), and he is a descendant of the royal line of the ancient Jewish king, David (v 32). Since David's reign ended, the Jewish people had waited nearly a thousand years for the promised new king who would rule like him. They were hoping for someone to release them from Roman oppression, but Jesus would be much more – he would rule eternally (v 33).

Jesus' mother was a virgin, but not because there's anything wrong with the natural method of human conception. In fact, there is a book in the Old Testament devoted to declaring how good and wonderful sex is in the context of marriage (Song of Songs). The virgin birth is the proof of Jesus' parentage. His mother was a young Jewish girl named Mary, and his father was the all-powerful God who created the world (v 35). Jesus came to rescue the human race with the power of God.

Respond *Mary asked the angel for more information (v 34) and then chose to believe (v 38). If there is anything about Christianity that you find hard to accept, don't be afraid to ask God honest questions. Speak to him now, asking him to help you understand. He will hear you.*

Seven hundred years in advance, a Jewish prophet predicted Jesus' unusual birth: Therefore the Lord himself will give you a sign: The virgin will be with child and will give birth to a son, and will call him Immanuel (which means: 'God with us'). (Isaiah 7:14)

15

Happy birthday to you

Prepare *At least one-third of the earth's population celebrates Christmas. Someone told someone else who told someone else… and finally even you and I heard about the birth of Jesus. You might like to thank God for that.*

Read Luke 2:1–14

[1] In those days Caesar Augustus issued a decree that a census should be taken of the entire Roman world. [2] (This was the first census that took place while Quirinius was governor of Syria.) [3] And everyone went to his own town to register. [4] So Joseph also went up from the town of Nazareth in Galilee to Judea, to Bethlehem the town of David, because he belonged to the house and line of David. [5] He went there to register with Mary, who was pledged to be married to him and was expecting a child. [6] While they were there, the time came for the baby to be born, [7] and she gave birth to her firstborn, a son. She wrapped him in cloths and placed him in a manger, because there was no room for them in the inn. [8] And there were shepherds living out in the fields near by, keeping watch over their flocks at night. [9] An angel of the Lord appeared to them, and the glory of the Lord shone around them, and they were terrified.

[10] But the angel said to them, "Do not be afraid. I bring you good news of great joy that will be for all the people. [11] Today in the town of David a Saviour has been born to you; he is Christ the Lord. [12] This will be a sign to you: You will find a baby wrapped in cloths and lying in a manger." [13] Suddenly a great company of the heavenly host appeared with the angel, praising God and saying, [14] "Glory to God in the highest, and on earth peace to men on whom his favour rests."

Explore Christmas can be a magical time of fantasy for both adults and children. In my city, Santa's workshops appear in department stores and familiar carols play over speaker systems. It can be easy to think it is all a pleasant seasonal fairy tale.

But Luke reports angels (vs 9,13), shepherds (v 8) and the baby in the manger (v 7) in almost the same breath as a census decreed by a specific Roman Caesar (v 1), when a specific governor was in power (v 2). The baby in a manger, the heavenly choir and the terrified shepherds are all anchored in time. In a small town in a quiet corner of the mighty Roman Empire, Jesus of Nazareth was born. This is no fairy tale. This is history.

Jesus turns the world upside down just by being born. The all-powerful Saviour of the world enters human life as a helpless baby. The great King from the royal line of David is born to poor parents, not in a palace, but in an animal shelter. The birth announcement is made not to world rulers but to lower-class shepherds (v 9). 'Heavenly host' (v 13) is a military term, but the most terrifying army in the universe comes proclaiming not war but peace (v 14). It is as though heaven has burst into earthly life with the birth of this child. Jesus' method of entry ignores everything our world values – wealth, power, privilege – so that he can show us what God really values: loving relationship between God and people.

Respond *The angel's 'good news of great joy' is for you too. Jesus was born to save you. Celebrate!*

Another ancient prediction: **For to us a child is born, to us a son is given, and the government will be on his shoulders. And he will be called Wonderful Counsellor, Mighty God, Everlasting Father, Prince of Peace. (Isaiah 9:6)**

Promises, promises

Prepare *We live in a world of unkept promises. Marriages that don't last 'till death do us part', face creams that don't remove wrinkles, jobs that fall through, politicians who change sides. It can make it hard for us to trust anyone or anything. Ask God to show you whether you can trust him.*

Read Luke 2:25–35

25 Now there was a man in Jerusalem called Simeon, who was righteous and devout. He was waiting for the consolation of Israel, and the Holy Spirit was upon him. 26 It had been revealed to him by the Holy Spirit that he would not die before he had seen the Lord's Christ. 27 Moved by the Spirit, he went into the temple courts. When the parents brought in the child Jesus to do for him what the custom of the Law required, 28 Simeon took him in his arms and praised God, saying: 29 "Sovereign Lord, as you have promised, you now dismiss your servant in peace. 30 For my eyes have seen your salvation, 31 which you have prepared in the sight of all people, 32 a light for revelation to the Gentiles and for glory to your people Israel." 33 The child's father and mother marvelled at what was said about him. 34 Then Simeon blessed them and said to Mary, his mother: "This child is destined to cause the falling and rising of many in Israel, and to be a sign that will be spoken against, 35 so that the thoughts of many hearts will be revealed. And a sword will pierce your own soul too."

Explore When God became a human being, he didn't do it on impulse. God had been planning the rescue of the human race ever since the first people tried to run the world their own way. He could have cut us off for ever for rejecting him, but instead he came after us, driven by his great love for us.

God's rescue plan involved one particular nation, the Jewish people. Over the course of perhaps 2,000 years, he made very special promises to them, about the way that God would use them to bring people from all nations to himself (v 32). All these promises were fulfilled in one very special Jew, Jesus (v 30). With the help of God, Simeon recognised in the tiny baby Jesus everything that righteous Jews had been waiting for (vs 25–27).

Jesus was a real person, born into a devout Jewish family (v 27). The other people we meet in the pages of the Bible are just as real. I wonder how the new mother must have felt to hear such great and such tragic news about her son in the same breath (vs 34,35). Simeon was bursting with the excitement of seeing all his hopes and expectations fulfilled. He could die happy (vs 26,29) now that he had seen what his people had been longing for.

Respond *Have you ever been hurt by someone else's failure to keep a promise? God keeps his promises. Open your heart to his promise to save you.*

> *Jesus was the answer to a promise God made about 2,000 years earlier to a man named Abraham, the father of the Jewish people:* 'I will make you into a great nation and I will bless you; I will make your name great, and you will be a blessing. I will bless those who bless you, and whoever curses you I will curse; and all peoples on earth will be blessed through you.' (Genesis 12:2,3)

day 4

Turn

Prepare *How do you react when people tell you that you've done something wrong? I usually feel awkward and embarrassed, and a bit defensive. However, sometimes I just have to confront my faults head-on, and that hurts! Ask God to help you to be brave enough and soft-hearted enough to hear what his Holy Spirit is trying to tell you today.*

Read Luke 3:15—22

John, the son of Mary's relatives, was out in the desert, calling people to turn from their wickedness and be baptised in the river. [15] The people were waiting expectantly and were all wondering in their hearts if John might possibly be the Christ. [16] John answered them all, "I baptise you with water. But one more powerful than I will come, the thongs of whose sandals I am not worthy to untie. He will baptise you with the Holy Spirit and with fire. [17] His winnowing fork is in his hand to clear his threshing floor and to gather the wheat into his barn, but he will burn up the chaff with unquenchable fire." [18] And with many other words John exhorted the people and preached the good news to them. [19] But when John rebuked Herod the tetrarch because of Herodias, his brother's wife, and all the other evil things he had done, [20] Herod added this to them all: He locked John up in prison. [21] When all the people were being baptised, Jesus was baptised too. And as he was praying, heaven was opened [22] and the Holy Spirit descended on him in bodily form like a dove. And a voice came from heaven: "You are my Son, whom I love; with you I am well pleased."

Explore   The last of the Jewish prophets is ready to announce the Messiah's arrival. A fiery preacher who called a spade a spade, John the Baptist didn't mind who he offended, even the adulterous king (vs 19,20). His outspokenness eventually cost him his life – beheaded at Herod's command. In contrast, ordinary people responded in droves to John's message, stricken by the news that they were on the wrong track and eager to turn back to God.

As for the rumours that John might be the expected deliverer, his dismissive response is basically: 'You ain't seen nothing yet' (vs 15,16). Enter Jesus, and heaven bursts open on this delightful and dearly loved Son of God (v 22). God pours himself into Jesus to empower him for the three tough years of ministry that lie ahead (v 22).

John points forward to an unpopular part of Jesus' job: judgement. The burning of chaff with unquenchable fire (v 17) hardly sounds like 'good news' (v 18) but, when you think about it, the destruction of evil and everything that hurts people *is* good news.

Baptism was a traditional Jewish way of showing a change of heart (repentance). Jesus commanded his followers to be baptised as a sign that their lives have turned around and that they now belong to him.

Respond *'Repentance' is a permanent part of the Christian life. Even once we've made the big turnaround to follow Jesus, he will nudge us to smaller changes in direction our whole life long. If you feel as though Jesus wants you to turn away from something in your life that doesn't please him, ask him to give you the strength to do it.*

> I urge you, brothers, in view of God's mercy, to offer your bodies as living sacrifices, holy and pleasing to God ... Do not conform any longer to the pattern of this world, but be transformed by the renewing of your mind. (Romans 12:1,2)

Resist temptation

Prepare *'I can resist everything except temptation,' said Oscar Wilde, but it's really no laughing matter. We can hurt ourselves and others by giving in to small and large temptations, from eating too much chocolate to having an affair with our best friend's spouse. Our relationship with God also suffers. Ask God to show you how to face temptation.*

Read Luke 4:1–13

¹ Jesus, full of the Holy Spirit, returned from the Jordan and was led by the Spirit in the desert, ² where for forty days he was tempted by the devil. He ate nothing during those days, and at the end of them he was hungry. ³ The devil said to him, "If you are the Son of God, tell this stone to become bread." ⁴ Jesus answered, "It is written: 'Man does not live on bread alone.'" ⁵ The devil led him up to a high place and showed him in an instant all the kingdoms of the world. ⁶ And he said to him, "I will give you all their authority and splendour, for it has been given to me, and I can give it to anyone I want to. ⁷ So if you worship me, it will all be yours." ⁸ Jesus answered, "It is written: 'Worship the Lord your God and serve him only.'" ⁹ The devil led him to Jerusalem and had him stand on the highest point of the temple. "If you are the Son of God," he said, "throw yourself down from here. ¹⁰ For it is written: "'He will command his angels concerning you to guard you carefully; ¹¹ they will lift you up in their hands, so that you will not strike your foot against a stone.'" ¹² Jesus answered, "It says: 'Do not put the Lord your God to the test.'" ¹³ When the devil had finished all this tempting, he left him until an opportune time.

Explore Out in the harsh Middle Eastern desert, after nearly six weeks without food (v 2), Jesus shows us the strength of his character. The devil's suggestion (v 3) sounds reasonable, but it is asking him to use his power for his own benefit, a frequent temptation for those in leadership. Jesus rejects the temptation by quoting the Bible (v 4): 'Man does not live on bread alone but on every word that comes from the mouth of the Lord' (Deuteronomy 8:3). A free and open relationship with God is more nourishing even than food to a starving man.

The second temptation is about power. The oppressive power of the day, the Roman Empire, was certainly on the devil's side, as, perhaps, are many of today's world governments (v 6). It must have been tempting for Jesus to see an opportunity to stop the oppression of his own people (v 7), but he recognised that, whatever the appearances, God was ultimately in charge (v 8).

The devil tries one last time, tempting Jesus to get God to prove himself (v 9). This time even the devil quotes the Bible (vs 10,11; Psalm 91:11,12)! But Jesus knows that to test God's promises in such a brazen way would be ultimately to say he didn't trust God (v 12).

In the end, Jesus refuses to be drawn to spectacular, self-serving or short-term answers. He is determinedly devoted to God's eternal purposes.

Respond *If you are struggling with temptation, ask Jesus to help you – he knows what it's like. If you have failed to resist, ask him to forgive you – he came because it is impossible for us to be perfect.*

Because he himself suffered when he was tempted, he is able to help those who are being tempted ... Let us then approach the throne of grace with confidence, so that we may receive mercy and find grace to help us in our time of need. (Hebrews 2:18; 4:16)

Who is this man?

Prepare *Our television screens nightly show our world's fascination with evil, and many people are looking for spooky experiences that take them beyond the everyday. However, the Bible declares that evil is not fun, and it isn't fantasy. If you have trouble accepting that there are evil spirits in the world, ask God to show you where he draws the line between superstition and spiritual fact. If your past experience has made you all too aware of evil forces, and have made you afraid, ask the Holy Spirit to convince you of his power to protect you.*

Read Luke 4:31—37

[31] Then [Jesus] went down to Capernaum, a town in Galilee, and on the Sabbath began to teach the people. [32] They were amazed at his teaching, because his message had authority. [33] In the synagogue there was a man possessed by a demon, an evil spirit. He cried out at the top of his voice, [34] "Ha! What do you want with us, Jesus of Nazareth? Have you come to destroy us? I know who you are – the Holy One of God!" [35] "Be quiet!" Jesus said sternly. "Come out of him!" Then the demon threw the man down before them all and came out without injuring him. [36] All the people were amazed and said to each other, "What is this teaching? With authority and power he gives orders to evil spirits and they come out!" [37] And the news about him spread throughout the surrounding area.

Explore Fresh from his battle with evil in the desert that we read about yesterday, Jesus begins establishing an astonishing ministry. He wasn't the only teacher travelling around the Jewish synagogues at that time, but Jesus stands out from the crowd. Jewish teachers quoted teachers of the past, but Jesus doesn't need to quote anyone else. He has the authority of God's Spirit (v 32). Exorcists of that period used elaborate spells and incantations to try to cast out an evil spirit, but Jesus doesn't need any mumbo-jumbo. His command is brief, direct and instantly effective (v 35).

The people are asking themselves the question: Who is this man? (vs 32,36). The demon, on the other hand, knows exactly who Jesus is (v 34). However, it doesn't do the demon any good. Knowledge is not the same thing as relationship. The demon's obedience to Jesus is that of a criminal forced at gunpoint into a police car, not the living obedience of true and loving relationship with God.

Respond *Do you want to really know this astonishing man, rather than just know about him? Jesus will open himself up to you if you ask him. Ask him to use his authority and power in your life – but be prepared for amazing things to happen!*

> *The Jewish prophet Daniel foresaw the power and authority of Jesus:* 'In my vision at night I looked, and there before me was one like a son of man, coming with the clouds of heaven. He approached the Ancient of Days [God] and was led into his presence. He was given authority, glory and sovereign power; all peoples, nations and men of every language worshipped him. His dominion is an everlasting dominion that will not pass away, and his kingdom is one that will never be destroyed.' (Daniel 7:13,14)

Awesome

Prepare *Imagine God's Holy Spirit like a breeze sweeping through your heart and mind, blowing away all your worries and distractions. Ask him to prepare you to meet the real Jesus.*

Read Luke 5:1–11

[1] One day as Jesus was standing by the Lake of Gennesaret, with the people crowding around him and listening to the word of God, [2] he saw at the water's edge two boats, left there by the fishermen, who were washing their nets. [3] He got into one of the boats, the one belonging to Simon, and asked him to put out a little from shore. Then he sat down and taught the people from the boat. [4] When he had finished speaking, he said to Simon, "Put out into deep water, and let down the nets for a catch." [5] Simon answered, "Master, we've worked hard all night and haven't caught anything. But because you say so, I will let down the nets." [6] When they had done so, they caught such a large number of fish that their nets began to break. [7] So they signalled to their partners in the other boat to come and help them, and they came and filled both boats so full that they began to sink. [8] When Simon Peter saw this, he fell at Jesus' knees and said, "Go away from me, Lord; I am a sinful man!" [9] For he and all his companions were astonished at the catch of fish they had taken, [10] and so were James and John, the sons of Zebedee, Simon's partners. Then Jesus said to Simon, "Don't be afraid; from now on you will catch men." [11] So they pulled their boats up on shore, left everything and followed him.

Explore Once again, Jesus is teaching (vs 1,3) and, once again, we end up asking: Who is this man? Today we also meet Simon Peter, who became a leader in the Christian church. But right now, he is a tired fisherman (v 5). The experienced professional listens to the carpenter's advice (v 5b); a sure sign that Peter recognised the authority of Jesus.

Peter was probably no worse than the next bloke. But just as most of us look best in soft lighting, most of us feel spiritually OK when we are with people who are about the same as us. For Peter, being in Jesus' presence shone a halogen searchlight into his very soul, revealing every flaw (v 8).

However, Jesus doesn't condemn him. He tells him to stop being scared, and what's more, he gives him a job to do (v 10). Peter and his friends dropped everything, and followed Jesus (v 11). Fishing was still a good occupation, but their priority at that moment was collecting people for God's kingdom.

Respond *Sometimes our unworthiness comes into sharp contrast with God's holiness and we grieve. However, when we feel bowed down by our sinfulness, God doesn't put his foot on us and hold us there – he gently lifts us up and gives us a worthwhile role to play. If you are feeling unworthy today, allow God to show you his love and compassion and purpose.*

The prophet Isaiah had a similar experience: 'Woe to me!' I cried. 'I am ruined! For I am a man of unclean lips … and my eyes have seen the King, the LORD Almighty.' Then one of the seraphs flew to me … and said, '… your guilt is taken away and your sin atoned for.' Then I heard the voice of the Lord saying, 'Whom shall I send? And who will go for us?' And I said, 'Here am I. Send me!' (Isaiah 6:5–8)

The forgiver

Prepare *Many people carry around burdens of guilt for something that happened in the past. For some of us it's a tiny little thing that no one else even remembers; for others, it can be quite major and even criminal. Whichever, it can strangle our relationships and even affect our health. If you are carrying guilt today, you might like to mime lifting it off your shoulders and placing it at the feet of Jesus, and wait to see what he will do with it as you read today's reading.*

Read Luke 5:18–26

[18] Some men came carrying a paralytic on a mat and tried to take him into the house to lay him before Jesus. [19] When they could not find a way to do this because of the crowd, they went up on the roof and lowered him on his mat through the tiles into the middle of the crowd, right in front of Jesus. [20] When Jesus saw their faith, he said, "Friend, your sins are forgiven." [21] The Pharisees and the teachers of the law began thinking to themselves, "Who is this fellow who speaks blasphemy? Who can forgive sins but God alone?" [22] Jesus knew what they were thinking and asked, "Why are you thinking these things in your hearts? [23] Which is easier: to say, 'Your sins are forgiven,' or to say, 'Get up and walk'? [24] But that you may know that the Son of Man has authority on earth to forgive sin. . . ." He said to the paralysed man, "I tell you, get up, take your mat and go home." [25] Immediately he stood up in front of them, took what he had been lying on and went home praising God. [26] Everyone was amazed and gave praise to God. They were filled with awe and said, "We have seen remarkable things today."

Explore In the days before wheelchairs, the only way for a paralysed person to get about was with the help of others. This man's friends are so determined to get him to Jesus that they take him up onto the flat roof of the house and dig their way through to lower him into the middle of the crowd (v 19). It must have caused quite a stir, but the thing that captures Jesus' attention is the faith of both the paralysed man and his friends (v 20). There are times when all of us need the support of believing friends to carry us, either because our faith or our bodies are not strong enough.

They've come for healing, but Jesus says, 'Your sins are forgiven' (v 20). It seems almost like a change of subject. Once again, we confront the question: Who is this man? This time it is asked by Jesus' opponents (v 21). They rightly recognise that God is the only one who can forgive sins, but they then assume that Jesus must be blaspheming. By the astonishing healing of the man (v 25), Jesus proves that he does indeed have God's authority (v 24).

Unforgiveness between people blocks relationship, and it's the same between us and God. Doctors can cure, but only Jesus can restore loving relationship with God. The physical healing of this man was fantastic, but his spiritual healing is a far greater thing.

Respond *Remember that burden of guilt we talked about? Allow Jesus to take it away from you, and praise God.*

Every person on this planet needs forgiveness, and God is the only one who can give it: **For as high as the heavens are above the earth, so great is his love for those who fear him; as far as the east is from the west, so far has he removed our transgressions [sins] from us. (Psalm 103:11,12)**

A generous spirit

Prepare *We live in a society whose catchphrase is 'What about my rights?' Today's reading is going to shake that philosophy to its foundations. Can you open yourself to Jesus' view of rights and responsibilities?*

Read Luke 6:27—38

Jesus said: [27] "But I tell you who hear me: Love your enemies, do good to those who hate you, [28] bless those who curse you, pray for those who mistreat you. [29] If someone strikes you on one cheek, turn to him the other also. If someone takes your cloak, do not stop him from taking your tunic. [30] Give to everyone who asks you, and if anyone takes what belongs to you, do not demand it back. [31] Do to others as you would have them do to you. [32] If you love those who love you, what credit is that to you? Even 'sinners' love those who love them. [33] And if you do good to those who are good to you, what credit is that to you? Even 'sinners' do that. [34] And if you lend to those from whom you expect repayment, what credit is that to you? Even 'sinners' lend to 'sinners', expecting to be repaid in full. [35] But love your enemies, do good to them, and lend to them without expecting to get anything back. Then your reward will be great, and you will be sons of the Most High, because he is kind to the ungrateful and wicked. [36] Be merciful, just as your Father is merciful. [37] Do not judge, and you will not be judged. Do not condemn, and you will not be condemned. Forgive, and you will be forgiven. [38] Give, and it will be given to you. A good measure, pressed down, shaken together and running over, will be poured into your lap. For with the measure you use, it will be measured to you."

Explore Jesus was a revolutionary. Sayings like 'do unto others …' and 'turn the other cheek' are now clichés, but they originally came from the mouth of Jesus Christ two thousand years ago (vs 29,31). We've lost sight of their shock value. The old Jewish law was 'an eye for an eye, and a life for a life'. God gave them this law partly to limit evil. For example, two Israelites once slaughtered a whole village because one resident had raped their sister. God introduced the rule that the punishment should fit the crime. But with the advent of Jesus, the Son of God, everything changes. There's no mention of 'rights', only responsibilities. Jesus' audience is told to love even enemies (vs 27,28). The time for payback is finished (v 29).

This is more than morality or behaviour. The focus is not on what the other person deserves, but on who we want to be. We are to be loving (vs 27,35), merciful and forgiving (vs 28,29,36,37), and generous in every sense (vs 30,35,37,38), so that we can become like our heavenly Father (vs 35–36). The saying could be reworded, 'do unto others as you'd like God to do unto you', or even 'be as you'd like God to be'. We don't deserve God's love, forgiveness or generosity, and we can be like him in showing love, forgiveness and generosity towards people who don't deserve it. This is desperately difficult, and we can only ever do it in the power of God's Holy Spirit.

Respond *Is there anyone who has hurt you deeply, whom you struggle to forgive? Ask God to help you to learn to love them, bit by bit.*

> Therefore, as God's chosen people, holy and dearly loved, clothe yourselves with compassion, kindness, humility, gentleness and patience. Bear with each other and forgive whatever grievances you may have against one another. Forgive as the Lord forgave you. (Colossians 3:12,13)

Foundations

Prepare *Queensland's Gold Coast has beautiful sandy beaches, lined with smart high-rise towers. The people who built them had to put down foundations a long, long way to reach the bedrock below the sand. As any engineer will tell you, it doesn't matter how beautiful the building is if the foundation won't hold. Building a good foundation for a life is just as crucial. We can add all sorts of colour and style to our existence, but it will fall in a heap if the foundation isn't strong enough. What is your life built upon?*

Read Luke 6:43—49

Jesus said: [43] "No good tree bears bad fruit, nor does a bad tree bear good fruit. [44] Each tree is recognised by its own fruit. People do not pick figs from thorn-bushes, or grapes from briers. [45] The good man brings good things out of the good stored up in his heart, and the evil man brings evil things out of the evil stored up in his heart. For out of the overflow of his heart his mouth speaks. [46] "Why do you call me, 'Lord, Lord,' and do not do what I say? [47] I will show you what he is like who comes to me and hears my words and puts them into practice. [48] He is like a man building a house, who dug down deep and laid the foundation on rock. When the flood came, the torrent struck that house but could not shake it, because it was well built. [49] But the one who hears my words and does not put them into practice is like a man who built a house on the ground without a foundation. The moment the torrent struck that house, it collapsed and its destruction was complete."

Explore Jesus says life is like gardening. If you want strawberries, don't plant cabbages (v 44) or you're bound to be disappointed (as will everyone who eats your jam!). If, like me, you ever regret things you've said, Jesus offers sound advice. What comes out of our mouths is what has gone into our hearts (v 45). What we say will be flavoured by what we read, watch and listen to. We need to actively and eagerly seek good input.

Jesus says life is like housing construction (vs 48,49). I once saw a house where the land had subsided, causing cracks and leaks. It was probably hard to tell the land wasn't going to hold firm. Sometimes, the things we have built our lives upon can look solid and dependable – a first-class job, a loving family. But then recession comes or someone dies, and it falls apart. Our lives need to be built to cyclone / earthquake standard, with the deepest and strongest foundation possible – relationship with God through Jesus.

The key is in verse 47. If we listen to Jesus' words to us through the Bible, absorb them into our hearts and live them out in our words and actions, we will be strong and fruitful Christians, even in the face of the worst hardship or the strongest opposition.

Respond *As you go through this day, think about what you are putting your trust in and what is going into your heart. Ask God to help you to anchor your life in him.*

Blessed is the man who trusts in the LORD, whose confidence is in him. He will be like a tree planted by the water that sends out its roots by the stream. It does not fear when heat comes; its leaves are always green. It has no worries in a year of drought and never fails to bear fruit. (Jeremiah 17:7,8)

Lord of creation

Prepare *I grew up in a sailing family, but still somehow managed to be afraid of water. Departing on time was not my family's forte, so we were regularly caught out in the vicious late afternoon storms that whipped the bay into a frenzy. I would scurry below decks, wrap myself in a huge yellow life jacket and pray. Hard! Today we're going to read about a group of 'sailors' who found themselves engulfed by a terrifying storm, but who were even more terrified by what stopped the storm. Take a deep breath, abandon your preconceptions about the 'meek and mild' Jesus and prepare to discover what it means for Jesus to be 'the boss'.*

Read Luke 8:22–25

22 One day Jesus said to his disciples, "Let's go over to the other side of the lake." So they got into a boat and set out. 23 As they sailed, he fell asleep. A squall came down on the lake, so that the boat was being swamped, and they were in great danger. 24 The disciples went and woke him, saying, "Master, Master, we're going to drown!" He got up and rebuked the wind and the raging waters; the storm subsided, and all was calm. 25 "Where is your faith?" he asked his disciples. In fear and amazement they asked one another, "Who is this? He commands even the winds and the water, and they obey him."

Explore Once again, Luke gets us asking that same question: Who *is* this man? There were other teachers around whose passionate speeches could draw large crowds. There were magicians who could perform impressive tricks, including apparent healings. But today's incident sets Jesus far apart from any of his contemporaries.

The lake of Galilee is renowned for its sudden storms. Winds sweep down from the surrounding mountains and in a moment a sunny day becomes a maelstrom.

Several of Jesus' disciples were professional fishermen, so storms couldn't have been a new experience for them. This storm must have been something special to throw these seasoned sailors into a panic.

Their words to Jesus (v 24) could mean several things. 'How can you sleep through this?'; 'Do something!' or even 'Get ready to swim for it!' Whatever the disciples were asking for, they clearly did not expect what they got – instant calm. Their terror transfers from the storm to Jesus, as they realise just who is in the boat with them. Only God can stop a storm.

Jesus rebukes not just the storm (v 24), but the disciples as well (v 25). His question might mean: 'Where has your faith gone?' Or it could mean: 'In what do you put your faith?' In either case, it is a challenge to stop trusting in their own ability as sailors and to trust the one who made the sea.

Respond *God is bigger than anything that could happen to you. If you are in the midst of a storm right now, ask him to hold you tight, to give you his peace and to guide you safely to the other side.*

> *The ancient poets of the Bible recognised that only God could control the weather:* O LORD God Almighty, who is like you? You are mighty, O LORD, and your faithfulness surrounds you. You rule over the surging sea; when its waves mount up, you still them. (Psalm 89:8,9)

Secrets

Prepare *I once encountered a young couple who had struggled for years to keep the husband's positive HIV status a secret. I think that I would have been overwhelmed simply by the practical problems of concealing the enormous amount of medication he had to swallow to a strict timetable each day. But the hardest part was surely battling through without the support and prayers of their church. Many of us are carrying secret burdens of one kind or another. If you've got a secret you just can't handle any more, ask God to show you a way forward as you read his message today.*

Read Luke 8:43–48

[42] As Jesus was on his way, the crowds almost crushed him. [43] And a woman was there who had been subject to bleeding for twelve years, but no one could heal her. [44] She came up behind him and touched the edge of his cloak, and immediately her bleeding stopped. [45] "Who touched me?" Jesus asked. When they all denied it, Peter said, "Master, the people are crowding and pressing against you." [46] But Jesus said, "Someone touched me; I know that power has gone out from me." [47] Then the woman, seeing that she could not go unnoticed, came trembling and fell at his feet. In the presence of all the people, she told why she had touched him and how she had been instantly healed. [48] Then he said to her, "Daughter, your faith has healed you. Go in peace."

Explore Just as Jesus is being crushed by the crowds (v 42), this woman has been crushed by her medical condition for twelve long years (v 43). She has suffered not just the physical impact of feeling drained and anaemic for all that time, but also the social impact. At this time, someone who was bleeding continuously was denied access to general society and religious fellowship. It's unlikely that this woman would have felt free to come up to Jesus during the normal public healings. So, in her desperation, she tries for a secret healing (v 44).

But there's not going to be a secret healing. Jesus demands that she declare herself (vs 45,46). In other instances, Jesus knew the thoughts in people's hearts, so he probably knew exactly who had touched him and why. His demand is not based on his need to know who it was, but on her need to own up.

Forced out of hiding, she tells the full story (v 47). It must have been embarrassing talking publicly about what was probably a 'women's problem', and it may have been against the rules for her even to be in that crowd. But with her public admission comes public vindication. Jesus wants her to have physical healing, social healing and, most importantly, spiritual healing (v 48).

Healing is a wonderful product of Jesus' ministry, and there are times even today when miraculous physical healings occur in Jesus' name. The most important thing is not the private impact of the healing, but the public impact of our faith.

Respond *If you are feeling weighed down by the pressures of health or relationship problems, ask God to lift you up. If you are nervous about declaring your new faith to family, friends and workmates, ask God to give you courage.*

The LORD is close to the broken-hearted and saves those who are crushed in spirit. (Psalm 34:18)

Who am I?

Prepare *Jesus is a popular guy in the twenty-first century. His concern for justice, his love for outsiders and his fearless opposition to the religious establishment all make him an icon for action groups in our society. They tend to view his death as a simple miscarriage of justice. In the general population, I talk to many people who have a vague and woolly idea that Jesus was a 'good man'. They usually haven't actually done any research on which to base their opinion. The most reliable source on Jesus' identity would have to be the man himself. Thanks to the Bible, we have a record of what Jesus said and did. Today we're going to discover who Jesus believed he was. Open your heart to God, and prepare to be challenged and inspired.*

Read Luke 9:18—22

[18] Once when Jesus was praying in private and his disciples were with him, he asked them, "Who do the crowds say I am?" [19] They replied, "Some say John the Baptist; others say Elijah; and still others, that one of the prophets of long ago has come back to life." [20] "But what about you?" he asked. "Who do you say I am?" Peter answered, "The Christ of God." [21] Jesus strictly warned them not to tell this to anyone. [22] And he said, "The Son of Man must suffer many things and be rejected by the elders, chief priests and teachers of the law, and he must be killed and on the third day be raised to life."

Explore This time Jesus himself is asking the 'Who is this man?' question (v 18). Just like us, Jesus' contemporaries had lots of different ideas about his identity (v 19). The story turns on Peter's revelation in verse 20. Peter's knowledge is not the product of rumours. It stems from a personal relationship with the man in question and insight given to Peter by God. The word 'Christ' is a Greek word meaning someone anointed by God with his Spirit for a special task. Jesus is not just *an* anointed one; he is *the* anointed one (v 20).

Although the disciples are right about this, Jesus warns them to keep it to themselves for now (v 21). The word 'Christ' had become politically loaded, so Jesus avoids it, generally preferring to call himself the 'Son of Man' (v 22). The Jews wanted the Christ to free them from the oppression of the Roman Empire, through a military victory. Jesus doesn't want to trigger a misplaced popular uprising, so he sets out to explain to his inner circle what is actually required of the Christ (v 22). It was puzzling and distressing news, and they never really understood it until after Jesus' death and resurrection. Put simply, the world's rejection of God earned it the death penalty. Because God loved us, Jesus took the penalty on our behalf. His resurrection is the sign that the plan worked.

Respond *It can take some time to fully grasp these mysterious truths, so if you're still puzzled, don't be afraid to talk to God about it.*

He was pierced for our transgressions, he was crushed for our iniquities; the punishment that brought us peace was upon him, and by his wounds we are healed. We all, like sheep, have gone astray, each of us has turned to his own way; and the LORD has laid on him the iniquity of us all. (Isaiah 53:5,6)

In denial

Prepare *Today's reading contains some lessons that are hard for us to learn. I am still learning them after twenty years as a Christian. A friend of mine who has been a Christian most of her life had tears in her eyes as she explained her struggle to follow this teaching of Jesus, and to work out exactly what it meant for her daily life. Try to open your heart to God as you enter today's reading, asking him to help you understand what this will mean for you. Remember that God is patient and that turning us into the people we can be is a life's work.*

Read Luke 9:23–26

23 Then [Jesus] said to them all: "If anyone would come after me, he must deny himself and take up his cross daily and follow me. 24 For whoever wants to save his life will lose it, but whoever loses his life for me will save it. 25 What good is it for a man to gain the whole world, and yet lose or forfeit his very self? 26 If anyone is ashamed of me and my words, the Son of Man will be ashamed of him when he comes in his glory and in the glory of the Father and of the holy angels."

Explore The disciples are having a tough time. Remember from yesterday how they'd just heard that the role of the Messiah was to suffer and die, rather than win a political victory? Well now they learn that their role is not to take power beside him in some military coup, but to follow their leader down the path of suffering and sacrifice (v 23).

Verse 24 contains echoes of martyrdom, and it certainly turned out that way for that small group gathered around Jesus. Many early church leaders died for their faith. For most of us in the western world, persecution is rarely fatal, but the principles still apply. I know a brilliant surgeon who could have revelled in luxury and prestige, but chose instead to take his (willing) young family off to a dirty and dangerous Third World country where he could use his medical skills to show God's love. To outsiders, it appears that he has lost his life for the sake of Jesus – but he tells of a life that is truly worth living. Jesus doesn't want just the available bits of us, or even the best bits. He wants everything. He wants to be more important to us than anything else in life. When that happens, we find true meaning and purpose.

Respond *More than once, I have struggled to give something up for God. Is there anything in your life that you would not be prepared to give up for the sake of Jesus? You might like to write it on a slip of paper and discuss it with God right now. Don't be afraid to tell him how you really feel. Try to be open to him. It may take some time.*

Paul was in prison for his faith when he wrote: I consider that our present sufferings are not worth comparing with the glory that will be revealed in us. (Romans 8:18)

Being busy vs just being

Prepare *Life is getting busier and busier, and every day seems full of distractions. You might like to jot down a list of the things that are on your mind. Imagine that Jesus, in the flesh, is sitting in a chair opposite you. Work through your list, one item at a time, telling Jesus everything that is good and bad about each one, as he listens with interest and compassion. Now take a few deep breaths and wait for his gentle reply.*

Read Luke 10:38—42

³⁸ As Jesus and his disciples were on their way, he came to a village where a woman named Martha opened her home to him. ³⁹ She had a sister called Mary, who sat at the Lord's feet listening to what he said. ⁴⁰ But Martha was distracted by all the preparations that had to be made. She came to him and asked, "Lord, don't you care that my sister has left me to do the work by myself? Tell her to help me!" ⁴¹ "Martha, Martha," the Lord answered, "you are worried and upset about many things, ⁴² but only one thing is needed. Mary has chosen what is better, and it will not be taken away from her."

Explore I confess I feel a little bit sorry for poor old Martha. The whole 'Jesus tour' has arrived on her doorstep (v 38), all needing to be fed and rested, and there's a lot to do to make that happen. She can't believe that Mary would be sitting down and leaving all the work to her (v 40).

There may be an element of challenging gender expectations here – in those days, women were supposed to do the housework and men were supposed to learn theology. But the main message of Jesus' reply (vs 41,42) seems to be that Martha's feverish activity has distracted her from what really matters (v 40). What Jesus would most like to be presented with is not a gourmet meal, but an open and teachable heart. The most important behaviour for a disciple of Jesus is not a lot of purposeful activity, but just *being* in his presence and listening.

Our actions do matter – as a sign of our response to Jesus' free gift of loving relationship with God. But in the end, Christianity is not about what we do, but who we are. If you have chosen to follow Jesus, you are a beloved child of the Lord of the universe, and that is worth just sitting and thinking about.

Respond *If you are a new Christian, you may have found that you instinctively want to do things that please Jesus and that's good, but make sure that you also take time out just to 'be'. Wallow in his presence and soak up his love for you. You might want to express yourself in poetry, painting or song.*

King David knew the joy of God's presence: One thing I ask of the LORD, this is what I seek: that I may dwell in the house of the LORD all the days of my life, to gaze upon the beauty of the LORD and to seek him in his temple. (Psalm 27:4)

How to pray

Prepare *Ask God to show you how to pray.*

Read Luke 11:1–13

¹ One day Jesus was praying in a certain place. When he finished, one of his disciples said to him, "Lord, teach us to pray, just as John taught his disciples." ² He said to them, "When you pray, say: 'Father, hallowed be your name, your kingdom come. ³ Give us each day our daily bread. ⁴ Forgive us our sins, for we also forgive everyone who sins against us. And lead us not into temptation.' " ⁵ Then he said to them, "Suppose one of you has a friend, and he goes to him at midnight and says, 'Friend, lend me three loaves of bread, ⁶ because a friend of mine on a journey has come to me, and I have nothing to set before him.' ⁷ "Then the one inside answers, 'Don't bother me. The door is already locked, and my children are with me in bed. I can't get up and give you anything.' ⁸ I tell you, though he will not get up and give him the bread because he is his friend, yet because of the man's boldness he will get up and give him as much as he needs. ⁹ "So I say to you: Ask and it will be given to you; seek and you will find; knock and the door will be opened to you. ¹⁰ For everyone who asks receives; he who seeks finds; and to him who knocks, the door will be opened. ¹¹ "Which of you fathers, if your son asks for a fish, will give him a snake instead? ¹² Or if he asks for an egg, will give him a scorpion? ¹³ If you then, though you are evil, know how to give good gifts to your children, how much more will your Father in heaven give the Holy Spirit to those who ask him!"

Explore Some people can make prayer seem like an incantation or a ritual, but Jesus' instructions on the subject were straightforward. It is a conversation based on intimate relationship, and Jesus gave a good example by his own constant prayerfulness (eg verse 1). He told his disciples what to pray, how to pray and what to expect. Verses 2–4 provide the basic structure of the Lord's Prayer, which has become well-known in many parts of the world. We are to ask for the world to know God (v 2), for the provision of our daily needs (v 3), that we might be forgiven and forgiving, and for help in avoiding temptation (v 4).

Verses 5–10 reveal the spirit in which we should pray. Jesus is not telling us that God is reluctant to get out of his warm bed to hear our requests. The focus of this little tale is *our* behaviour, not God's. We are to be persistent and bold in asking God for what we need (vs 8–10), persevering until we reach a resolution.

Verses 9–13 tell us what to expect, based on the character of God, not our worthiness. If the average human father won't give a child something poisonous when they're hungry, how much more can we expect of an all-good, all-loving Father God? God is a generous Father who delights in giving good things to his children. God's idea of good won't always coincide with ours, however. I might have happily eaten chocolate all day as a child, but thankfully my mother gave me meat and bread and vegetables. In the same way, God will give us what is best for us. His best ever gift is the Holy Spirit (v 13).

Respond *Confidently ask God for the things he has told you to ask for.*

· Be joyful always; pray continually; give thanks in all circumstances,
· for this is God's will for you in Christ Jesus.
· (1 Thessalonians 5:16–18)
·
·
·
·
·
·
·

Never fear

Prepare *Our society often portrays God as a benevolent, white-bearded old man who sits in heaven just waiting to bestow indulgent smiles on his naughty but lovable children. Their God is harmless and ineffectual. He is nothing like the God of the Bible. Ask the Holy Spirit to help you feel the magnitude of his holiness right now, in the depths of your soul.*

Read Luke 12:1–7

[1] Meanwhile, when a crowd of many thousands had gathered, so that they were trampling on one another, Jesus began to speak first to his disciples, saying: "Be on your guard against the yeast of the Pharisees, which is hypocrisy. [2] There is nothing concealed that will not be disclosed, or hidden that will not be made known. [3] What you have said in the dark will be heard in the daylight, and what you have whispered in the ear in the inner rooms will be proclaimed from the roofs. [4] I tell you, my friends, do not be afraid of those who kill the body and after that can do no more. [5] But I will show you whom you should fear: Fear him who, after the killing of the body, has power to throw you into hell. Yes, I tell you, fear him. [6] Are not five sparrows sold for two pennies? Yet not one of them is forgotten by God. [7] Indeed, the very hairs of your head are all numbered. Don't be afraid; you are worth more than many sparrows."

Explore I've been afraid of lots of things in my life. Spiders. Oversleeping on an exam day. Mosquito-borne diseases. Muggers in dark alleys. My fears have varying levels of relevance to actual life. However, today's lesson from Jesus is that even the things that are worth being afraid of are nothing, compared to God.

The greatest human fear is death (v 4), but Jesus points out that even a murderer's power is limited. They can take the life from your body, but they can't have any impact on your eternity. Only God will decide your eternal fate, and his power is absolute (v 5). He is the only one worth fearing. He hates hypocrisy, which seeps into every part of life, like yeast through a lump of dough (v 1). To say one thing and do another might fool people for a time, but God is not fooled, and the day is coming when every two-faced person will be exposed for all the world to see (vs 2,3).

But the astonishingly good news is that this fearsome God is on our side (vs 6,7). He knows everything about you, even the number of hairs on your head, and still he treasures you.

Respond *Our God is no old dodderer sitting on a cloud. He is very scary indeed. But he also has a fierce and protective love for you. Spend a little time in quiet reverence, soaking up this amazing truth.*

The prophet Isaiah understood that God is not 'safe', but he is our only safe haven: The Lord said: 'Do not call conspiracy everything that these people call conspiracy; do not fear what they fear, and do not dread it. The Lord Almighty is the one you are to regard as holy, he is the one you are to fear, he is the one you are to dread, and he will be a sanctuary.' (Isaiah 8:11–14)

day 18

No worries

Prepare *Worry can gnaw away at us, sapping our strength and draining all the joy from life. No wonder that Jesus tells us not to do it! But still I sometimes struggle with worry, and maybe you do too. If you're worried about anything today, ask God to fill you with his peace. Imagine the Holy Spirit flooding through you like soothing warm water, surging into every corner of your being, washing away your fears.*

Read Luke 12:15,23–26,29–34

[15] Then [Jesus] said to them, "Watch out! Be on your guard against all kinds of greed; a man's life does not consist in the abundance of his possessions. [23] Life is more than food, and the body more than clothes. [24] Consider the ravens: They do not sow or reap, they have no storeroom or barn; yet God feeds them. And how much more valuable you are than birds! [25] Who of you by worrying can add a single hour to his life? [26] Since you cannot do this very little thing, why do you worry about the rest? [29] And do not set your heart on what you will eat or drink; do not worry about it. [30] For the pagan world runs after all such things, and your Father knows that you need them. [31] But seek his kingdom, and these things will be given to you as well. [32] Do not be afraid, little flock, for your Father has been pleased to give you the kingdom. [33] Sell your possessions and give to the poor. Provide purses for yourselves that will not wear out, a treasure in heaven that will not be exhausted, where no thief comes near and no moth destroys. [34] For where your treasure is, there your heart will be also."

Explore First-century society was just as focused on wealth and possessions as ours is today (v 30). Jesus declares what many a millionaire has realised on his deathbed: We are not defined by what we own (v 15) and money can't buy the breath of life (v 25).

Compared to grasping after more and greater possessions, worrying about not being able to pay the electricity bill might seem to be in a totally different category, but Jesus groups them together. Both pursuing wealth and fearing poverty involve setting our sights on something other than Jesus. The message is that, whether we own much or little in the material sense, Christians are all fabulously wealthy in the spiritual sense. We own something infinitely precious that can never depreciate or be taken away from us (v 33). We are beloved children of God, heirs of the King of the universe (v 32). We are to be responsible citizens of this world, but our focus is on citizenship of another world.

Jesus' advice to hold lightly to our possessions can also apply to other areas of life. We can frantically pursue good health, family togetherness, career goals. And conversely, we can worry incessantly about the lack of such things. Either approach is to make a god of something other than Jesus.

Respond *Most of us struggle at times against materialism, whether we are rich or poor. You might like to mime handing over your possessions and your money worries to God, and ask him to help you leave them there. If you feel that God is calling you to give something away, you might like to discuss it with a mature Christian whom you respect.*

> *King David knew both wealth and poverty, but God remained his deepest longing:* As the deer pants for streams of water, so my soul pants for you, O God. My soul thirsts for God, for the living God. (Psalm 42:1,2)

Expect opposition

Prepare *In a church in a former communist country, I sat on a hard wooden bench next to people who had spent many years in mental asylums for their faith, betrayed by their own family members. They had clung tenaciously to Jesus through every attempt to make them let go – and he had hung on just as firmly to them. These people truly knew the value of relationship with Jesus, and I was deeply challenged by them. If anyone or anything is trying to make you let go of Jesus, ask God to hang on to you.*

Read Luke 12:49—53

Jesus said: [49] "I have come to bring fire on the earth, and how I wish it were already kindled! [50] But I have a baptism to undergo, and how distressed I am until it is completed! [51] Do you think I came to bring peace on earth? No, I tell you, but division. [52] From now on there will be five in one family divided against each other, three against two and two against three. [53] They will be divided, father against son and son against father, mother against daughter and daughter against mother, mother-in-law against daughter-in-law and daughter-in-law against mother-in-law."

Explore If you're facing opposition after having decided to follow Jesus, please understand that this doesn't mean there's something wrong with you. All Christians face opposition at some time in our lives. Depending on the culture, persecution can include anything from teasing and contempt, to loss of job opportunities and marriage prospects, or even death. Jesus came to bring peace between God and humankind, but this very action created hostility between people (v 51). This is because those who want to pursue peace with God are travelling in a completely opposite direction to those who don't, and friction results.

Jesus suffered the ultimate persecution. The baptism of fire that he is anticipating (vs 49,50) is his death on the cross. This is how Jesus would deal with every single action of rejection or rebellion against God since the beginning of the world. A woman longs for the birth of her baby, even though labour is painful and unpleasant, because there will be a cherished child at the end of it. In an even more powerful way, Jesus longs for his sacrificial death to come, even though it will be a horrifying experience, because the end result will be the salvation of the world.

Respond *I don't know what opposition you might be facing, but Jesus does. Ask him for strength. If you are holding back from committing yourself to Jesus because you're afraid of how others might react, ask God for courage and wisdom.*

This writer was in constant danger because of his faith: If God is for us, who can be against us? For I am convinced that neither death nor life, neither angels nor demons, neither the present nor the future, nor any powers, neither height nor depth, nor anything else in all creation, will be able to separate us from the love of God that is in Christ Jesus our Lord. (Romans 8:31,38,39)

day 20

One way

Prepare *Christianity, or God's kingdom, is a bit like a warm, bright house, spilling light out into a cold, dark place. Often people will circle the house for years, looking in the windows, and yearning for the love and relationships that are inside. There is only one door. It stands open and Jesus is at the door, holding out his arms in welcome. But sometimes people are afraid he'll ask them to leave some of their baggage at the door, so they stay out in the cold. The day will come when the door is shut and the blinds drawn. If you're still circling, please don't be outside then.*

Read Luke 13:23—30

23 Someone asked him, "Lord, are only a few people going to be saved?" He said to them, 24 "Make every effort to enter through the narrow door, because many, I tell you, will try to enter and will not be able to. 25 Once the owner of the house gets up and closes the door, you will stand outside knocking and pleading, 'Sir, open the door for us.' But he will answer, 'I don't know you or where you come from.' 26 Then you will say, 'We ate and drank with you, and you taught in our streets.' 27 But he will reply, 'I don't know you or where you come from. Away from me, all you evildoers!' 28 There will be weeping there, and gnashing of teeth, when you see Abraham, Isaac and Jacob and all the prophets in the kingdom of God, but you yourselves thrown out. 29 People will come from east and west and north and south, and will take their places at the feast in the kingdom of God. 30 Indeed there are those who are last who will be first, and first who will be last."

Explore Someone asks Jesus whether only the best people are going to be saved (v 23). Jesus dismisses this spiritual snobbery with a straightforward answer containing three unpalatable truths.

Firstly, he says there is only one way into God's kingdom. Jesus is both the narrow door (v 24) and the owner of the house – the owner is the one who 'taught in our streets' (v 26). Secondly, he says that some people who think they'll be 'in' have a surprise coming (v 30). Being a good Jew (or a good churchgoer) is no entry pass. Brushing past Jesus on the way through life doesn't qualify. Only those who actually *know* Jesus will be admitted to heaven (v 27). Thirdly, he says that being outside of heaven is not the fun get-together that some people joke about, but a place of torment and regret (v 28).

I find these truths troubling, because I want everybody to go to heaven. But the thing is, God put that desire in my heart because it's what he wants too. He wants everybody to come in and have a loving relationship with him, but he won't force them. And, if God hadn't sent Jesus, there would have been *no* way in.

Respond *If you've been brushing past Jesus for years, get to know him, starting now. If you are finding it hard to accept that Jesus is the only way to God, talk to him honestly about it.*

> *Jesus said:* 'Trust in God; trust also in me. In my Father's house are many rooms; if it were not so, I would have told you. I am going there to prepare a place for you … I will come back and take you to be with me that you also may be where I am. I am the way and the truth and the life. No-one comes to the Father except through me.' (John 14:1–3,6)

Counting the cost

Prepare *Have you ever done anything that was truly worthwhile? What did it cost you? Think about not just finances, but time, relationships or other opportunities that you sidelined in order to pursue the goal. How much are you prepared to give up in order to pursue life with Jesus?*

Read Luke 14:26–33

Jesus said: [26] "If anyone comes to me and does not hate his father and mother, his wife and children, his brothers and sisters – yes, even his own life – he cannot be my disciple. [27] And anyone who does not carry his cross and follow me cannot be my disciple. [28] Suppose one of you wants to build a tower. Will he not first sit down and estimate the cost to see if he has enough money to complete it? [29] For if he lays the foundation and is not able to finish it, everyone who sees it will ridicule him, [30] saying, 'This fellow began to build and was not able to finish.' [31] Or suppose a king is about to go to war against another king. Will he not first sit down and consider whether he is able with ten thousand men to oppose the one coming against him with twenty thousand? [32] If he is not able, he will send a delegation while the other is still a long way off and will ask for terms of peace. [33] In the same way, any of you who does not give up everything he has cannot be my disciple."

Explore These words from Jesus are shocking, and he means them to be. He wants to jolt us into realising that he must be the most important thing in our lives. Christian faith cannot work any other way. We must let go of everything else that we thought was important, in order to give Jesus central place (v 33).

Jesus is not saying that we should behave cruelly towards our family any more than he is saying we should construct a large wooden cross and drag it around with us every day (v 27). The Bible must always be read in context, and in other places Jesus tells us that we are to care for our family members in a godly way. (As he was dying, Jesus even made arrangements for one of his disciples to care for his mother.) Rather, he is using a figure of speech to make his point. Our love for Jesus should be so strong that our love for our family and even our own lives looks like hate in comparison (v 26).

Sometimes this love will override other things that we might have liked to do. Jesus wants to be more important to us than even the most precious and beautiful things of this life. Do not become a follower of Jesus without counting the cost.

Respond *If you are willing, symbolically hand over to Jesus all the things you treasure most and wait to see what he will return to you.*

- *Paul was a highly respected member of the community… until he chose Jesus and became an outlaw:* But whatever was to my profit I now consider loss for the sake of Christ. What is more, I consider everything a loss compared to the surpassing greatness of knowing Christ Jesus my Lord, for whose sake I have lost all things. I consider them rubbish, that I may gain Christ. (Philippians 3:7,8)

day 22

You are precious!

Prepare *The story goes that a man dropped his car keys at night and was hunting for them under a streetlight. A passer-by stopped to help and asked, 'Where exactly did you drop them?' 'Over there,' the man said, pointing into the darkness. 'Then why are we looking over here?' asked his puzzled helper. 'Because there's more light over here,' the man replied. My natural inclination is to stay in my comfort zone, but the challenge from Jesus is to go to the darkest and dirtiest places in the world to search for lost people.*

Read Luke 15:1–10

[1] Now the tax collectors and "sinners" were all gathering around to hear him. [2] But the Pharisees and the teachers of the law muttered, "This man welcomes sinners and eats with them." [3] Then Jesus told them this parable: [4] "Suppose one of you has a hundred sheep and loses one of them. Does he not leave the ninety-nine in the open country and go after the lost sheep until he finds it? [5] And when he finds it, he joyfully puts it on his shoulders [6] and goes home. Then he calls his friends and neighbours together and says, 'Rejoice with me; I have found my lost sheep.' [7] I tell you that in the same way there will be more rejoicing in heaven over one sinner who repents than over ninety-nine righteous persons who do not need to repent. [8] Or suppose a woman has ten silver coins and loses one. Does she not light a lamp, sweep the house and search carefully until she finds it? [9] And when she finds it, she calls her friends and neighbours together and says, 'Rejoice with me; I have found my lost coin.' [10] In the same way, I tell you, there is rejoicing in the presence of the angels of God over one sinner who repents."

Explore Jesus spent a lot of time in the company of undesirable people. They were drawn to him, like iron filings to a magnet (v 1), and he did not send them away. The religious leaders were far from happy about this (v 2). To their way of thinking, a religious teacher and community leader should not encourage friendships with people whose morals were questionable. Jesus was setting a bad example. Imagine a modern-day archbishop being seen socialising with prostitutes and drug dealers.

However, Jesus answers their criticism, as he so often does, with stories. In these stories, the people 'who do not need to repent' (v 7; compare the sheep of v 4) are being aligned with the Pharisees. They think they're OK. Jesus is out to find the people who know they're lost and want to be found. He is not endorsing sinful behaviour but revealing the yearning heart of God. He is ecstatic when one person turns back to him.

There are many examples in the Bible where people with doubtful pasts turned to Jesus and started over again. There are similar examples in life today. You may be one of them. Whatever your past, you are exquisitely precious to God.

Respond *If you have turned to God, there has been a party in heaven in celebration (v 10). Allow yourself to feel God's joy today.*

- *God told the prophet Isaiah how much he yearned for people who were far from worthy:* 'I revealed myself to those who did not ask for me; I was found by those who did not seek me. To a nation that did not call on my name, I said, 'Here am I, here am I.' All day long I have held out my hands to an obstinate people, who walk in ways not good, pursuing their own imaginations.' (Isaiah 65:1,2)

Forgiven, forgiving

Prepare *I recently read the story of a woman who held her husband as he died, during a terrible massacre in Tasmania. She struggled with anger and hatred for some time, but eventually felt compelled to forgive the murderer, because of what God's forgiveness had meant to her. She says that since then she has begun to heal and she now even prays for the man. Hers is a remarkable and challenging story. If there is a deep hurt weighing on you today, release it into God's strong and capable hands. You can trust him with it. Ask the Holy Spirit to show you how you can be healed.*

Read Luke 17:1—6

[1] Jesus said to his disciples: "Things that cause people to sin are bound to come, but woe to that person through whom they come. [2] It would be better for him to be thrown into the sea with a millstone tied around his neck than for him to cause one of these little ones to sin. [3] So watch yourselves. If your brother sins, rebuke him, and if he repents, forgive him. [4] If he sins against you seven times in a day, and seven times comes back to you and says, 'I repent,' forgive him." [5] The apostles said to the Lord, "Increase our faith!" [6] He replied, "If you have faith as small as a mustard seed, you can say to this mulberry tree, 'Be uprooted and planted in the sea,' and it will obey you."

Explore Christians are members of a family, with responsibilities towards each other. Jesus tells us not to lead each other astray (vs 1,2) and to let each other know when we've made a mistake (v 3). It can be very hard to know when to be silent and when to speak up, and it's an issue that needs lots of prayer. We earn the right to advise someone else by being genuinely involved in their lives. If in doubt, seek the counsel of more mature Christians.

We have an even more difficult responsibility to forgive each other (vs 3,4).

Christians are not perfect and we do hurt each other, sometimes very deeply. When we choose to forgive, we're not saying that the person's hurtful action doesn't matter. We're refusing to retaliate and deciding deliberately not to hang on to our pain. Bitterness and the desire for vengeance are natural human reactions, but they alienate us from each other and spoil our relationship with God.

Just like us, the disciples realise that forgiveness will be a difficult task, and they ask Jesus to increase their faith so they might be equal to the challenge (v 5). However, Jesus has a double-edged answer. You don't need a huge faith, just get on and do it; but you'll also be surprised how much a small faith can achieve (v 6).

Respond *If you need to forgive or ask for forgiveness, see if you can find the courage to confront it. If it is very hard, tell God so, and ask him to help you.*

- *Jesus doesn't ask us to do anything he hasn't already done:* When they came to the place called the Skull, there they crucified him, along with the criminals – one on his right, the other on his left. Jesus said, 'Father, forgive them, for they do not know what they are doing.' (Luke 23:33,34)

No regrets!

Prepare *When I was a young journalist, I went to a press conference for Torvill and Dean, the ice dancers. I was trying not to look too excited and overawed, and desperately wanted to ask for an autograph, but I was afraid the experienced and cynical journalists around me would sneer. So I didn't do it. I've always been sorry about that — but at least it was only an autograph! Don't let peer pressure stop you grabbing hold of the things that will really matter for the rest of your life.*

Read Luke 18:35—43

³⁵ As Jesus approached Jericho, a blind man was sitting by the roadside begging. ³⁶ When he heard the crowd going by, he asked what was happening. ³⁷ They told him, "Jesus of Nazareth is passing by." ³⁸ He called out, "Jesus, Son of David, have mercy on me!" ³⁹ Those who led the way rebuked him and told him to be quiet, but he shouted all the more, "Son of David, have mercy on me!" ⁴⁰ Jesus stopped and ordered the man to be brought to him. When he came near, Jesus asked him, ⁴¹ "What do you want me to do for you?" "Lord, I want to see," he replied. ⁴² Jesus said to him, "Receive your sight; your faith has healed you."
⁴³ Immediately he received his sight and followed Jesus, praising God. When all the people saw it, they also praised God.

Explore I love this man's story. He knew what he wanted, he knew who could get it for him and he just went for it! In his era, physical disability was the ticket to a life of poverty and disadvantage (v 35). We don't know how long this man had been blind, but he's obviously had plenty of experience of being sidelined and considered unimportant. We don't know why the crowd told him to be quiet (v 39). Perhaps they thought it was undignified; perhaps they thought a man in his lowly social position had no right to push himself forward; perhaps, since some people at that time even believed that illness or disability was a punishment for sin, they thought he was too sinful to be calling on Jesus.

Unbowed by public opinion, he refuses to be silenced (v 39). This man stands out from the crowd in more ways than one. It's his faith that brings the healing (v 42), and that faith is in the Son of David (vs 38,39). This was another name for the Jewish Messiah. Jesus' response is virtually a confirmation that the blind man's title for him is correct. A blind beggar can see what the Pharisees cannot! Despite all their education and privilege, they are spiritually blind and have failed to see who Jesus is. The man shows his understanding of the healing by his response. He follows Jesus and gives glory to God (v 43).

Respond *Don't let anything hold you back from following Jesus. Don't worry what anyone else will think. Just call out to Jesus.*

> *Jesus said:* 'The kingdom of heaven is like a merchant looking for fine pearls. When he found one of great value, he went away and sold everything he had and bought it.' (Matthew 13:45,46)

Identity parade

Prepare *As a small child, I remember screaming my head off while my mother ran round the house stuffing newspaper into our leaky windows, to 'stop the cyclone getting in'. I thought the cyclone was a monster coming to attack us. Looking back, both my definition of a cyclone and my faith in bits of newspaper to stop it had one or two flaws! Many people have the same trouble correctly identifying Jesus. Ask him to show you who he is and why it matters.*

Read Luke 19:35–44

[35] They brought [the colt] to Jesus, threw their cloaks on the colt and put Jesus on it. [36] As he went along, people spread their cloaks on the road. [37] When he came near the place where the road goes down the Mount of Olives, the whole crowd of disciples began joyfully to praise God in loud voices for all the miracles they had seen: [38] "Blessed is the king who comes in the name of the Lord!" "Peace in heaven and glory in the highest!" [39] Some of the Pharisees in the crowd said to Jesus, "Teacher, rebuke your disciples!" [40] "I tell you," he replied, "if they keep quiet, the stones will cry out." [41] As he approached Jerusalem and saw the city, he wept over it [42] and said, "If you, even you, had only known on this day what would bring you peace – but now it is hidden from your eyes. [43] The days will come upon you when your enemies will build an embankment against you and encircle you and hem you in on every side. [44] They will dash you to the ground, you and the children within your walls. They will not leave one stone on another, because you did not recognise the time of God's coming to you."

Explore Jesus now enters Jerusalem and the final days of his life. He knows he is heading for execution – the Jewish leaders have put out a warrant for his arrest –

but he enters the city anyway. The colt (v 35) fulfilled a direct prophecy (see the quotation from the book of Zechariah below) that would have been well known to Jesus' Jewish followers. The miracles have shown that Jesus is the Messiah (v 37), and the colt confirms it. They fail to recognise, however, that the colt is also a sign that he is coming in peace (a king heading into battle would have ridden a warhorse, not a young donkey). Their nationalistic hopes have become caught up in their religious hopes. They want the Messiah to get rid of Roman oppression and taxes. The Pharisees realise that the commotion could draw unfavourable attention from the Roman guards and urge Jesus to quieten the crowd (v 39), but he tells them that there's no way to put a lid on it (v 40).

The crowd's failure to get it right was to have tragic consequences for Jesus, when several days later their joyful cries turned to ugly shouts of 'Crucify him!' It was also to have tragic consequences for the Jewish people in AD 70, when Jesus' prediction about the destruction of Jerusalem (vs 43,44) was to prove hauntingly accurate. The failure to recognise Jesus has consequences.

Respond *Jesus is indeed the king. King of the universe, king of the future and of the past. Ask him to help you to truly allow him to be king of your life today.*

:
:
:
:
:
:
:
:
:

This event was predicted ahead of time: Rejoice greatly, O Daughter of Zion! Shout, Daughter of Jerusalem! See, your king comes to you, righteous and having salvation, gentle and riding on a donkey, on a colt, the foal of a donkey … He will proclaim peace to the nations. (Zechariah 9:9,10)

Apocalypse now?

Prepare *The end of the world is a popular topic for writers and film-makers, but a bit of an awkward one for many Christians. So many cults have predicted the end of the world – without success – that even to raise the subject smacks of the lunatic fringe. But it was a vital topic to Jesus. Ask God to show you his plans for the future of our planet.*

Read Luke 21:7,8,10,11,16–19,25–28

Jesus told his disciples the temple would be destroyed: [7] "Teacher," they asked, "when will these things happen? And what will be the sign that they are about to take place?" [8] He replied: "Watch out that you are not deceived. For many will come in my name, claiming, 'I am he,' and, 'The time is near.' Do not follow them." [10] Then he said to them: "Nation will rise against nation, and kingdom against kingdom. [11] There will be great earthquakes, famines and pestilences in various places, and fearful events and great signs from heaven. [16] You will be betrayed even by parents, brothers, relatives and friends, and they will put some of you to death. [17] All men will hate you because of me. [18] But not a hair of your head will perish. [19] By standing firm you will gain life. [25] There will be signs in the sun, moon and stars. On the earth, nations will be in anguish and perplexity at the roaring and tossing of the sea. [26] Men will faint from terror, apprehensive of what is coming on the world, for the heavenly bodies will be shaken. [27] At that time they will see the Son of Man coming in a cloud with power and great glory. [28] When these things begin to take place, stand up and lift up your heads, because your redemption is drawing near."

Explore It seems the news is full of wars and natural disasters (vs 10, i 1). There are many countries on earth today where being a Christian is illegal and even fatal (vs 16,17). However, it's also true that such things have been going on since Jesus spoke these words – they tend to run in cycles. It's very hard to tell whether the global upheaval we're seeing on our television screens is the exact one referred to by Jesus in this discussion.

There are a number of things we can be certain of, however. Jesus will return from heaven and the whole earth will see it (v 27). Anyone who tries to pin down a date for this is going directly against Jesus' word (v 8): 'No one knows about that day or hour, not even the angels in heaven, nor the Son, but only the Father' (Matthew 24:36). It will be a good day for those who know Jesus (vs 18,19,28). It will be a bad day for people who have rejected Jesus (v 26; see also quote below), and everything evil will be destroyed.

Respond *These words from Jesus can be frightening and upsetting because we don't want anyone to be destroyed. Take comfort from the fact that Jesus will look after you, and allow your fears to prompt you to pray earnestly for family and friends who have not yet understood who Jesus is.*

> *There will be an end and a new beginning:* 'Surely the day is coming; it will burn like a furnace. All the arrogant and every evildoer will be stubble, and that day that is coming will set them on fire,' says the LORD Almighty. 'Not a root or a branch will be left to them. But for you who revere my name, the sun of righteousness will rise with healing in its wings. And you will go out and leap like calves released from the stall.' (Malachi 4:1,2)

day 27

Flesh and blood

Prepare *I once took part in a communion service in eastern Europe and was overwhelmed by the sensation of being part of a global family, all united around the table of Jesus, regardless of geography or time zones or cultures. You are a special part of God's family. Thank him, and pray for your brothers and sisters around the world.*

Read Luke 22:8,13—22

[8] Jesus sent Peter and John, saying, "Go and make preparations for us to eat the Passover." *He gave them detailed instructions on how to find the right house.* [13] They left and found things just as Jesus had told them. So they prepared the Passover. [14] When the hour came, Jesus and his apostles reclined at the table. [15] And he said to them, "I have eagerly desired to eat this Passover with you before I suffer. [16] For I tell you, I will not eat it again until it finds fulfilment in the kingdom of God." [17] After taking the cup, he gave thanks and said, "Take this and divide it among you. [18] For I tell you I will not drink again of the fruit of the vine until the kingdom of God comes." [19] And he took bread, gave thanks and broke it, and gave it to them, saying, "This is my body given for you; do this in remembrance of me." [20] In the same way, after the supper he took the cup, saying, "This cup is the new covenant in my blood, which is poured out for you. [21] But the hand of him who is going to betray me is with mine on the table.
[22] The Son of Man will go as it has been decreed, but woe to that man who betrays him."

Explore If you knew you were going to die tomorrow, what would you do tonight? The night before his crucifixion, Jesus and his disciples gather to eat the Passover meal (v 8); a commemoration of how God had miraculously freed the Jewish people from slavery in Egypt thousands of years ago. Jesus has some essential things to teach them, and time is running out. He knows that a close friend is about to turn him in, with fatal results (v 21), but this is part of the plan (v 22). Jesus is about to do something new (v 20), far beyond the scope of the original Passover, that will bring about the kingdom of God everyone has been waiting for (v 16). The next agonising hours will lead to freedom from slavery to sin and death for all of his followers until the end of time.

This meal is famously known as the Last Supper, and it is repeated according to Jesus' command (v 19) in Christian churches around the world today. To talk of eating Jesus' body (v 19) and drinking his blood (v 20) may sound gruesome, but it is not some kind of symbolic cannibalism. It is a sign that we identify with the death of Jesus and want to take into our beings the forgiveness his death has won for us. It is something that we do together (v 17) to show that we are all part of Christ.

Respond *Different churches have different 'personalities' and this shows in the way they celebrate the Lord's Supper. It can be very formal or very relaxed, but we are all remembering the one event. If you have an opportunity to take part in a communion service, meditate on the fact that Jesus died for you.*

- For whenever you eat this bread and drink this cup, you proclaim the Lord's death until he comes. (1 Corinthians 11:26)

day 28

Try, try, try again

Prepare *Past failures can haunt us and the fear of failure can stop us going after the things that are really important to us. Jesus has a different view of failure. Open your heart to him. He has something to tell you.*

Read Luke 22:31–34,54–62

During the meal, Jesus said: [31] "Simon, Simon, Satan has asked to sift you as wheat. [32] But I have prayed for you, Simon, that your faith may not fail. And when you have turned back, strengthen your brothers." [33] But he replied, "Lord, I am ready to go with you to prison and to death." [34] Jesus answered, "I tell you, Peter, before the cock crows today, you will deny three times that you know me." *Jesus was betrayed by Judas in the Garden of Gethsemane.* [54] Then seizing [Jesus], they led him away and took him into the house of the high priest. Peter followed at a distance. [55] But when they had kindled a fire in the middle of the courtyard and had sat down together, Peter sat down with them. [56] A servant girl saw him seated there in the firelight. She looked closely at him and said, "This man was with him." [57] But he denied it. "Woman, I don't know him," he said. [58] A little later someone else saw him and said, "You also are one of them." "Man, I am not!" Peter replied. [59] About an hour later another asserted, "Certainly this fellow was with him, for he is a Galilean." [60] Peter replied, "Man, I don't know what you're talking about!" Just as he was speaking, the cock crowed. [61] The Lord turned and looked straight at Peter. Then Peter remembered the word the Lord had spoken to him: "Before the cock crows today, you will disown me three times." [62] And he went outside and wept bitterly.

Explore I constantly thank God for the truthfulness of the Bible. Peter became a key leader of the early Christian church. It would have been so easy for the historians to massage the facts a little and make Peter look good. But, no, his failure is laid down in stark, uncompromising detail. At the Last Supper, Peter is full of bravado, so certain that he will go to death and back rather than desert his Lord (v 33). Just a few short hours later, in the chill early morning after a confusing and frightening night, Peter fails utterly. His piercing grief at his own weakness (v 62) is something I have identified with a number of times in the course of my Christian life.

The good news for Peter, and for us, is that Jesus did not leave him there in his desolation. After Jesus' resurrection, he restored Peter (see quote below). Just as Peter failed three times, there is a threefold challenge from Jesus. This is not a taunt, but a determination to cut to the heart of the pain and show Peter the way forward. Yes, he has failed, but he is still on the team.

Respond *We usually mean well, but sometimes we fail. If God is asking you to face up to failure today, confront it head on, but be gentle with yourself, just as Jesus is. He longs to restore you.*

> Jesus said to Simon Peter, 'Simon son of John, do you truly love me more than these?' 'Yes, Lord,' he said, 'you know that I love you.' Jesus said, 'Feed my lambs.' *Jesus asked again, with the same response.* The third time he said to him, 'Simon son of John, do you love me?' Peter was hurt because Jesus asked him the third time, 'Do you love me?' He said, 'Lord, you know all things; you know that I love you.' Jesus said, 'Feed my sheep.' (John 21:15–17)

day 29

Wrong reaction, right people

Prepare *A good friend of mine was coming to visit. As I watched for a woman with shoulder-length blonde hair to walk off the plane, I was forced to peer around a woman with short dark hair who was getting in the way. It was my friend! My blindness made us laugh. Failure to recognise Jesus, however, is no laughing matter.*

Read Luke 22:47,48,66—71; 23:8—11

⁴⁷ While [Jesus] was still speaking a crowd came up, and the man who was called Judas, one of the Twelve, was leading them. He approached Jesus to kiss him, ⁴⁸ but Jesus asked him, "Judas, are you betraying the Son of Man with a kiss?" ⁶⁶ At daybreak the council of the elders of the people, both the chief priests and teachers of the law, met together, and Jesus was led before them.

⁶⁷ "If you are the Christ," they said, "tell us." Jesus answered, "If I tell you, you will not believe me, ⁶⁸ and if I asked you, you would not answer. ⁶⁹ But from now on, the Son of Man will be seated at the right hand of the mighty God." ⁷⁰ They all asked, "Are you then the Son of God?" He replied, "You are right in saying I am." ⁷¹ Then they said, "Why do we need any more testimony? We have heard it from his own lips." *They took Jesus to the governor, Pilate, who sent him to King Herod.* ²³:⁸ When Herod saw Jesus, he was greatly pleased, because for a long time he had been wanting to see him. From what he had heard about him, he hoped to see him perform some miracle. ⁹ He plied him with many questions, but Jesus gave him no answer. ¹⁰ The chief priests and the teachers of the law were standing there, vehemently accusing him. ¹¹ Then Herod and his soldiers ridiculed and mocked him. Dressing him in an elegant robe, they sent him back to Pilate.

Explore Here we have three totally wrong reactions to Jesus, all from people who should have known better. Judas Iscariot, one of Jesus' inner circle, should have known who Jesus was, but he betrayed him to the Jews for the infamous thirty pieces of silver (22:47,48). We don't know why he did it, but perhaps he was frustrated by Jesus' failure to generate a military uprising.

The Jewish religious leaders (22:66) were always poring over the Scriptures and should have picked up on the prophecies that proved who Jesus was. But they were prejudiced against him from the start and were convinced that he must be lying. They thought they had the evidence to put him to death (22:71); they didn't stop to consider that he might actually be telling the truth (22:70).

King Herod was the Jewish civic leader, who should have had the interests of the Jewish people at heart. But he wants to see some magic tricks (23:8) and, when he doesn't get what he wants, like a petulant child he makes fun of the Lord of the universe and helps to send Jesus on to his death (23:11).

Sometimes people say that if they'd lived at the same time as Jesus, they wouldn't have so much trouble believing. But the truth is that belief stems from the heart, not the eyes and ears.

Respond *Chances are, you're reading this book because you want to know who Jesus is. Ask him to help you know him for who he really is. He loves to receive requests like that.*

> *God reaches out to his people to save them, and their rejection causes him profound grief: 'Woe to them, because they have strayed from me! Destruction to them, because they have rebelled against me! I long to redeem them but they speak lies against me.' (Hosea 7:13)*

Right reaction, wrong people

Prepare *Try to still your mind as you prepare to read about the death of Jesus.*

Read Luke 23:32–47

32 Two other men, both criminals, were also led out with him to be executed.
33 When they came to the place called the Skull, there they crucified him, along with the criminals – one on his right, the other on his left. 34 Jesus said, "Father, forgive them, for they do not know what they are doing." And they divided up his clothes by casting lots. 35 The people stood watching, and the rulers even sneered at him. They said, "He saved others; let him save himself if he is the Christ of God, the Chosen One." 36 The soldiers also came up and mocked him. They offered him wine vinegar 37 and said, "If you are the king of the Jews, save yourself." 38 There was a written notice above him, which read: THIS IS THE KING OF THE JEWS. 39 One of the criminals who hung there hurled insults at him: "Aren't you the Christ? Save yourself and us!" 40 But the other criminal rebuked him. "Don't you fear God," he said, "since you are under the same sentence? 41 We are punished justly, for we are getting what our deeds deserve. But this man has done nothing wrong." 42 Then he said, "Jesus, remember me when you come into your kingdom." 43 Jesus answered him, "I tell you the truth, today you will be with me in paradise." 44 It was now about the sixth hour, and darkness came over the whole land until the ninth hour, 45 for the sun stopped shining. And the curtain of the temple was torn in two. 46 Jesus called out with a loud voice, "Father, into your hands I commit my spirit." When he had said this, he breathed his last. 47 The centurion, seeing what had happened, praised God and said, "Surely this was a righteous man."

Explore This is the darkest day in the history of the world – even the sun stopped shining (vs 44,45). As he struggles to draw his last breaths, people are still criticising Jesus. Their theme is 'you saved others so save yourself!' (vs 35,37,39). But the fact is that, in order to save others, he had to refuse to save himself. The other 'savings' were temporary – all those people still died eventually. Someone had to absorb all the poison of several millennia of human rejection of God to provide a way out of eternal death and Jesus is soaking it up into himself here on the cross.

Only two people come close to understanding that. The first is a convicted criminal, who's done something bad enough to earn the death penalty. He has no chance to make amends, but simply because of his expression of faith (v 42), Jesus tells him he'll see him in heaven later (v 43). The second person is a Roman centurion, a Gentile who knew nothing of the Jewish God or the expected Messiah. But, as he watches Jesus die, he recognises him and praises God (v 47).

Respond *Some people find the extent of Jesus' forgiveness offensive, but the good news is, if he could forgive a condemned criminal, he can forgive you and me. Whatever you may have done, Jesus' death is enough. Thank him.*

> *Long before Jesus was born, this chillingly accurate prophecy was made: All who see me mock me; they hurl insults, shaking their heads: 'He trusts in the LORD; let the LORD rescue him. Let him deliver him, since he delights in him.' ... Dogs have surrounded me; a band of evil men has encircled me, they have pierced my hands and my feet. I can count all my bones; people stare and gloat over me. They divide my garments among them and cast lots for my clothing. (Psalm 22:7,8,16–18)*

Alive!

Prepare *Death is the final frontier. Occasionally, people who have been resuscitated report 'near-death experiences', but resurrection is a different matter. Only one man has ever died and returned immortal, never to die again. What would you like to ask this man, if you had the chance?*

Read Luke 23:55 — 24:11

[55] The women who had come with Jesus from Galilee followed Joseph and saw the tomb and how his body was laid in it. [56] Then they went home and prepared spices and perfumes. But they rested on the Sabbath in obedience to the commandment. [24:1] On the first day of the week, very early in the morning, the women took the spices they had prepared and went to the tomb. [2] They found the stone rolled away from the tomb, [3] but when they entered, they did not find the body of the Lord Jesus. [4] While they were wondering about this, suddenly two men in clothes that gleamed like lightning stood beside them. [5] In their fright the women bowed down with their faces to the ground, but the men said to them, "Why do you look for the living among the dead? [6] He is not here; he has risen! Remember how he told you, while he was still with you in Galilee: [7] 'The Son of Man must be delivered into the hands of sinful men, be crucified and on the third day be raised again.'" [8] Then they remembered his words. [9] When they came back from the tomb, they told all these things to the Eleven and to all the others. [10] It was Mary Magdalene, Joanna, Mary the mother of James, and the others with them who told this to the apostles. [11] But they did not believe the women, because their words seemed to them like nonsense.

Explore These women are at the end of their tether. For three years they have followed an amazing man who seemed to have the answer to the world's problems, only to see him falsely accused in a kangaroo court, then brutally executed without any resistance. Imagine the depth of their grief as they approach the tomb to care tenderly for the body of their Lord (v 1). When they get there, they find that the tomb has apparently been desecrated (v 2) and the body exhumed without permission (v 3). While they are still absorbing this shock, two extremely scary men appear (v 4) with a very confusing message (vs 5–7). I think by this stage I probably would have just fainted and been done with it! But, thankfully, these women somehow hold it together, and manage to remember and start to unravel the explanations of Jesus that had made no sense at the time (vs 7,8). When they get back to the others with the astounding good news (v 9), they are treated like a bunch of silly women (v 11). Tomorrow we'll see what happens next.

Respond *If you find the resurrection hard to get your mind around, don't despair. It seriously messed with the minds of the first witnesses to it. However, they came to understand that it was exactly what centuries of prophets and Jesus himself had said would happen. Come before Jesus with an open heart and ask him to help you understand.*

> *Before his death, Jesus had told his disciples:* 'We are going up to Jerusalem, and everything that is written by the prophets about the Son of Man will be fulfilled. He will be handed over to the Gentiles. They will mock him, insult him, spit on him, flog him and kill him. On the third day he will rise again.' The disciples did not understand any of this. (Luke 18:31–34)

Without a doubt

Prepare *If someone told you they'd seen a miracle, what proof would you want?*

Read Luke 24:36—49; Acts 1:3

³⁶ While they were still talking about this, Jesus himself stood among them and said to them, "Peace be with you." ³⁷ They were startled and frightened, thinking they saw a ghost. ³⁸ He said to them, "Why are you troubled, and why do doubts rise in your minds? ³⁹ Look at my hands and my feet. It is I myself! Touch me and see; a ghost does not have flesh and bones, as you see I have." ⁴⁰ When he had said this, he showed them his hands and feet. ⁴¹ And while they still did not believe it because of joy and amazement, he asked them, "Do you have anything here to eat?" ⁴² They gave him a piece of broiled fish, ⁴³ and he took it and ate it in their presence. ⁴⁴ He said to them, "This is what I told you while I was still with you: Everything must be fulfilled that is written about me in the Law of Moses, the Prophets and the Psalms." ⁴⁵ Then he opened their minds so they could understand the Scriptures. ⁴⁶ He told them, "This is what is written: The Christ will suffer and rise from the dead on the third day, ⁴⁷ and repentance and forgiveness of sins will be preached in his name to all nations, beginning at Jerusalem. ⁴⁸ You are witnesses of these things. ⁴⁹ I am going to send you what my Father has promised; but stay in the city until you have been clothed with power from on high." ^{1:3} After his suffering, he showed himself to these men and gave many convincing proofs that he was alive. He appeared to them over a period of forty days and spoke about the kingdom of God.

Explore Jesus' disciples knew for a certainty that he was dead. Then women had come back from the tomb with some wild story that Jesus was alive again, but they had put it down to hysteria. After all, it had been a very difficult few days for everyone. Now here he is, standing among them (v 36). I think, if I had seen a friend die and three days later he came into the room and started talking to me, I'd be just as scared as these disciples were (v 37). This is very weird. But Jesus is patient. He knows it will take some time for the truth to sink in. And he graciously invites them to touch and see (vs 39,40), and even offers to eat something (vs 41–43), since that is something a ghost can't do.

But this was not a one-off occurrence that could be passed off as an hallucination from the depths of grief. Jesus continued to prove himself for nearly six weeks, teaching them as he went along (Acts 1:3). He made absolutely certain that they would understand what his death and resurrection were all about. They had to be clear on the facts, because they were to be the historic witnesses (v 48), empowered by God (v 49).

The resurrection is not an optional extra. Without it, Christianity is nothing more than a moral code. Death and separation from God was the consequence of human sin and, in dying, Jesus shouldered that consequence for everyone who belongs to him. In his resurrection, he has beaten death. Because he rose, we too can have eternal life.

Respond *If you have doubts, take them honestly to God. He can cope. But be assured that this is history, not fantasy.*

: If you confess with your mouth, 'Jesus is Lord,' and believe in your
: heart that God raised him from the dead, you will be saved.
: (Romans 10:9)
:
:
:

day 33

Waiting

Prepare *Waiting can be one of the hardest things to do, but it can also be a special time of anticipation – a pregnant woman waiting for her baby, a child waiting for Christmas, a couple waiting for their wedding day. The disciples are waiting for their lives to be turned upside down.*

Read Acts 1:4–11

⁴ On one occasion, while [Jesus] was eating with them, he gave them this command: "Do not leave Jerusalem, but wait for the gift my Father promised, which you have heard me speak about. ⁵ For John baptised with water, but in a few days you will be baptised with the Holy Spirit." ⁶ So when they met together, they asked him, "Lord, are you at this time going to restore the kingdom to Israel?" ⁷ He said to them: "It is not for you to know the times or dates the Father has set by his own authority. ⁸ But you will receive power when the Holy Spirit comes on you; and you will be my witnesses in Jerusalem, and in all Judea and Samaria, and to the ends of the earth." ⁹ After he said this, he was taken up before their very eyes, and a cloud hid him from their sight.

¹⁰ They were looking intently up into the sky as he was going, when suddenly two men dressed in white stood beside them. ¹¹ "Men of Galilee," they said, "why do you stand here looking into the sky? This same Jesus, who has been taken from you into heaven, will come back in the same way you have seen him go into heaven."

Explore Numerous times before his death, Jesus discussed with his disciples the fact that he would have to go away, but that he would leave someone else in his place to look after them. He meant the Holy Spirit (v 5). They still don't really understand what that means, but they will soon.

The disciples also haven't yet understood that the goal is not political freedom (v 6). Jesus tells them to leave that up to God (v 7) and firmly changes their focus. Much more than the future of Israel is at stake. The Holy Spirit will empower them to testify about Jesus, not just to Jews (Jerusalem and Judea), but to Samaria (a despised neighbour) and the whole world (v 8).

Jesus is then taken up into 'heaven'. We don't know the geography of heaven, but we do know that it is where God's powerful presence is clearly visible. We know that Jesus is representing us there before God, a little like a lawyer acting on our behalf. We also know that Jesus is coming back (v 11).

God the Father, Jesus the Son and the Holy Spirit are three different persons, but somehow all the one God. This is one of the great mysteries of the Christian faith. Even God is a community of relationship.

Respond *The life, death and resurrection of Jesus Christ is good news, designed to be shared. Ask God to help you tell others what you have discovered.*

- *After he rose from the dead, Jesus gave a command to his disciples:* 'All authority in heaven and on earth has been given to me. Therefore go and make disciples of all nations, baptising them in the name of the Father and of the Son and of the Holy Spirit, and teaching them to obey everything I have commanded you. And surely I am with you always, to the very end of the age.' (Matthew 28:18–20)

The turning point

Prepare *There have been times when I have felt shy and reluctant to talk about my relationship with God. But there have been times when the words have just poured out of my mouth, with a passion and a clarity that astonishes me. That is the kind of thing the Holy Spirit does, when we let him. Ask God to help you understand what his Holy Spirit wants to do in your life.*

Read Acts 2:1–13

¹ When the day of Pentecost came, they were all together in one place. ² Suddenly a sound like the blowing of a violent wind came from heaven and filled the whole house where they were sitting. ³ They saw what seemed to be tongues of fire that separated and came to rest on each of them. ⁴ All of them were filled with the Holy Spirit and began to speak in other tongues as the Spirit enabled them. ⁵ Now there were staying in Jerusalem God-fearing Jews from every nation under heaven. ⁶ When they heard this sound, a crowd came together in bewilderment, because each one heard them speaking in his own language. ⁷ Utterly amazed, they asked: "Are not all these men who are speaking Galileans? ⁸ Then how is it that each of us hears them in his own native language? ⁹ Parthians, Medes and Elamites; residents of Mesopotamia, Judea and Cappadocia, Pontus and Asia, ¹⁰ Phrygia and Pamphylia, Egypt and the parts of Libya near Cyrene; visitors from Rome ¹¹ (both Jews and converts to Judaism); Cretans and Arabs – we hear them declaring the wonders of God in our own tongues!" ¹² Amazed and perplexed, they asked one another, "What does this mean?" ¹³ Some, however, made fun of them and said, "They have had too much wine."

Explore 'Pentecost' was a Jewish festival marking fifty days after the Passover festival (v 1), but it has become part of the Christian vocabulary because of what happened that first Pentecost after Jesus' death and resurrection. This is a turning point in world history. Before this, people with a special role to fulfil for God would be empowered by his Spirit for that particular task, but now, all Christians are indwelt by the Holy Spirit – all the time.

This doesn't mean God 'operates' us like remote-control puppets. Our spirit and the Holy Spirit dwell side by side, and he will not force his will on us. But we can hand over our lives to God, asking him to guide us by his Spirit and allow us to be part of his purposes for the world. The outcome, on this inaugural occasion, was that Jesus' followers spoke in languages they had never learned. A bunch of country boys from Galilee (v 7) suddenly spouted forth in every cosmopolitan language imaginable (vs 9,10). The result? The audience heard about the wonders of God (v 11). From this day forward, everyone baptised in the name of Jesus receives the Holy Spirit.

Respond *If you are a Christian, the Holy Spirit lives in you and will empower you to declare the wonders of God – if you let him. Just as some people ridiculed the disciples and said they were drunk (v 13), people will sometimes laugh at you for witnessing in the power of the Holy Spirit. Do it anyway.*

> *Ahead of time, God said:* 'And afterwards, I will pour out my Spirit on all people. Your sons and daughters will prophesy, your old men will dream dreams, your young men will see visions. Even on my servants, both men and women, I will pour out my Spirit in those days … And everyone who calls on the name of the LORD will be saved.' (Joel 2:28,29,32)

Stabbed in the heart

Prepare *Sometimes our mistakes can be heartbreaking – for ourselves as well as others. Jesus offers a fresh start. Ask him to show you how to begin again.*

Read Acts 2:14,22–24,32,36–42

[14] Then Peter stood up with the Eleven, raised his voice and addressed the crowd: [22] "Men of Israel, listen to this: Jesus of Nazareth was a man accredited by God to you by miracles, wonders and signs, which God did among you through him, as you yourselves know. [23] This man was handed over to you by God's set purpose and foreknowledge; and you, with the help of wicked men, put him to death by nailing him to the cross. [24] But God raised him from the dead, freeing him from the agony of death, because it was impossible for death to keep its hold on him. [32] God has raised this Jesus to life, and we are all witnesses of the fact. [36] Therefore let all Israel be assured of this: God has made this Jesus, whom you crucified, both Lord and Christ." [37] When the people heard this, they were cut to the heart and said to Peter and the other apostles, "Brothers, what shall we do?" [38] Peter replied, "Repent and be baptised, every one of you, in the name of Jesus Christ for the forgiveness of your sins. And you will receive the gift of the Holy Spirit. [39] The promise is for you and your children and for all who are far off – for all whom the Lord our God will call." [40] With many other words he warned them; and he pleaded with them, "Save yourselves from this corrupt generation." [41] Those who accepted his message were baptised, and about three thousand were added to their number that day. [42] They devoted themselves to the apostles' teaching and to the fellowship, to the breaking of bread and to prayer.

Explore This powerful sermon from Peter follows immediately after the disciples' fiery experience of the Holy Spirit that we read about yesterday. That extraordinary display of linguistics has created a captive audience. The teaching of Jesus in the weeks after his resurrection now stands Peter in good stead. He explains various Bible predictions and the way Jesus fulfils them (if you have a Bible, you can read them in the full text of this chapter of Acts). He is adamant that death could not keep Jesus in its clutches (vs 24,32), because Jesus is the Lord of life (v 36). He is clear that the execution of Jesus was not a violation of God's plan, but the fulfilment of it (v 23). This does not make the people any less responsible for Jesus' death (vs 23,36).

When the people hear that they have participated in the murder of the one they had waited so long to see, it strikes them like a physical agony (v 37). They want to make up for what they've done, but what could they possibly do? The startling answer is not a pronouncement of punishment, but the offer of a new life, in intimate relationship with God (v 38). Three thousand people responded immediately and were baptised, but it wasn't a shallow response soon forgotten. It changed the whole structure of their lives (v 42).

Respond *Jesus died for you. Turn to him and ask him to turn your life around.*

> *Jesus said:* 'For God so loved the world that he gave his one and only Son, that whoever believes in him shall not perish but have eternal life. For God did not send his Son into the world to condemn the world, but to save the world through him.'
> (John 3:16,17)

All together now

Prepare *A friend of mine lost two of her toes in a boating accident, and she found it hard to balance as a result. Even though they were such tiny parts of the body to lose — ones that people rarely see — they were an important part of life. The church of Jesus is like a body. He is the head, controlling where we go and why, and we are all the other bits, with different roles and responsibilities. When every part is working well, it buzzes with life. When any part suffers, all of it feels the impact. Being a Christian gives you significance and a place to belong. Think about that for a while, thanking Jesus. If this stirs up any painful feelings for you, perhaps to do with belonging, share them with God.*

Read Acts 2:42–47

[42] They devoted themselves to the apostles' teaching and to the fellowship, to the breaking of bread and to prayer. [43] Everyone was filled with awe, and many wonders and miraculous signs were done by the apostles. [44] All the believers were together and had everything in common. [45] Selling their possessions and goods, they gave to anyone as he had need. [46] Every day they continued to meet together in the temple courts. They broke bread in their homes and ate together with glad and sincere hearts, [47] praising God and enjoying the favour of all the people. And the Lord added to their number daily those who were being saved.

Explore This is 'church in action'. A church is not a building or even an organisation. It is a family of believers. We all need each other if we are going to function correctly. Christians differ as to whether it's still appropriate to live together in a type of commune (vs 44,45), and this is a description rather than a command. It clearly strengthened the fledgling church at the time that it was forming and bolstered it against the intense persecution that was to come.

The principles of their community are certainly still relevant today. We need to hear the apostles' teaching (v 42) through reading the Bible and hearing it explained, so that we can grow in confidence and understanding of our faith. Jesus commanded us to break bread together in the Lord's Supper or communion, and told us how to pray. Miracles will still happen sometimes, according to God's purposes (v 43). We still need to put the pressing needs of others before our own comfort (v 45). We need to meet together for encouragement and growth, fellowship with each other over meals (v 46), give praise to God and be good citizens (v 47). We need to obey Jesus' command to reach out to people who don't yet know him (v 47).

Respond *You need the love and support of other Christians as you follow Jesus, and they need your love and support. If you don't know how to go about finding a church, Soul Survivor or Scripture Union may be able to help you.*

Let us hold unswervingly to the hope we profess, for he who promised is faithful. And let us consider how we may spur one another on towards love and good deeds. Let us not give up meeting together, as some are in the habit of doing, but let us encourage one another – and all the more as you see the Day approaching. (Hebrews 10:23–25)

Boldly go

Prepare *Ask the Holy Spirit to give you the courage to be his person.*

Read Acts 4:10–13,19,24,27–31

Peter healed a crippled man in the name of Jesus, and he and John were jailed. The next day, the Jewish leaders gathered to question them and, filled with the Holy Spirit, Peter replied: [10] "It is by the name of Jesus Christ of Nazareth, whom you crucified but whom God raised from the dead, that this man stands before you healed. [11] He is 'the stone you builders rejected, which has become the capstone.' [12] Salvation is found in no one else, for there is no other name under heaven given to men by which we must be saved." [13] When they saw the courage of Peter and John and realised that they were unschooled, ordinary men, they were astonished and they took note that these men had been with Jesus. *They commanded them not to teach in the name of Jesus.* [19] But Peter and John replied, "Judge for yourselves whether it is right in God's sight to obey you rather than God." *Peter and John went back to the other believers, and they all prayed together.* [24] "Sovereign Lord," they said, "you made the heaven and the earth and the sea, and everything in them. [27] Herod and Pontius Pilate met together with the Gentiles and the people of Israel in this city to conspire against your holy servant Jesus, whom you anointed. [28] They did what your power and will had decided beforehand should happen. [29] Now, Lord, consider their threats and enable your servants to speak your word with great boldness. [30] Stretch out your hand to heal and perform miraculous signs and wonders through the name of your holy servant Jesus." [31] After they prayed, the place where they were meeting was shaken. And they were all filled with the Holy Spirit and spoke the word of God boldly.

Explore Can this be the same Peter who shrank in fear on the night of Jesus' betrayal? Now he is risking his life to proclaim Jesus' death and resurrection. The difference is the Holy Spirit, who now empowers Peter to do things he never thought possible.

Peter seems to have done most of the talking, but John was there too, and his quiet support is just as valuable as Peter's eloquence. Peter and John were firm on the facts of their faith (v 10), and they knew the Bible well enough to quote it back to professional Bible teachers (v 11). The Christians prayed for courage under fire, reminding themselves of God's 'bigness' (v 24) and his unassailable plan (v 28). We can learn from their example how to face up to opposition to our faith: keep the company of other Christians, know our Bibles, pray hard and remember who God is. I think I might have wanted to pray for protection, but they pray for boldness to talk all the more (v 29)!

Peter became a key leader in the early Christian church, and we can read some of his letters that have been recorded in the New Testament. He was still very human and made other mistakes in the course of his life. But in the power of the Holy Spirit he could do remarkable things for God.

Respond *Pray for Christians you know or have heard of who are being persecuted for their faith.*

> *Jesus told his disciples:* 'They will deliver you to synagogues and prisons, and you will be brought before kings and governors, and all on account of my name. This will result in your being witnesses to them. But make up your mind not to worry beforehand how you will defend yourselves. For I will give you words and wisdom that none of your adversaries will be able to resist or contradict.' (Luke 21:12–15)

The Damascus road

Prepare *Do you ever wonder where your life is headed? Ask Jesus to show you the way.*

Read Acts 9:3—9,15—20

A man named Saul set out to arrest believers on behalf of the Jewish leaders. [3] As he neared Damascus on his journey, suddenly a light from heaven flashed around him. [4] He fell to the ground and heard a voice say to him, "Saul, Saul, why do you persecute me?" [5] "Who are you, Lord?" Saul asked. "I am Jesus, whom you are persecuting," he replied. [6] "Now get up and go into the city, and you will be told what you must do." [7] The men travelling with Saul stood there speechless; they heard the sound but did not see anyone. [8] Saul got up from the ground, but when he opened his eyes he could see nothing. So they led him by the hand into Damascus. [9] For three days he was blind, and did not eat or drink anything. *God told a believer named Ananias to go and heal Saul, but Ananias was afraid.* [15] But the Lord said to Ananias, "Go! This man is my chosen instrument to carry my name before the Gentiles and their kings and before the people of Israel. [16] I will show him how much he must suffer for my name." [17] Then Ananias went to the house and entered it. Placing his hands on Saul, he said, "Brother Saul, the Lord – Jesus, who appeared to you on the road as you were coming here – has sent me so that you may see again and be filled with the Holy Spirit." [18] Immediately, something like scales fell from Saul's eyes, and he could see again. He got up and was baptised, [19] and after taking some food, he regained his strength. [20] At once he began to preach in the synagogues that Jesus is the Son of God.

Explore If you've ever heard anyone refer to a 'Damascus Road experience', this is the original. It is a total change of life direction for a brilliant young Pharisee named Saul (history knows him better by his other name, Paul). There are two examples of fear in this story, and two corresponding examples of Spirit-empowered boldness. Paul fell to the ground in terror when the light from heaven flashed around him (v 4). Ananias' knees went weak when God told him to help the infamous man who had been throwing Christians into prison. Ananias believed God and went boldly into the lion's den (v 17), even daring to call this fearsome man 'brother'. Paul went straight out and began vigorously expounding the very religion he had so brutally tried to stop (v 20). Both of them acted from their conviction that Jesus was Lord of all creation, the Son of God (vs 5,20).

I wonder what Paul's thoughts were in those three days of darkness (v 9), as he waited to see what would become of him (v 6). Instead of punishment, God sent healing and the gift of his Holy Spirit (v 17). This vicious opponent of the faith turned out to be God's secret weapon, taking the good news of Jesus to non-Jews (v 15). Paul used his education to good effect, and his many letters recorded in the New Testament even help us today to understand our faith.

Respond *Grace is an 'undeserved free gift', and that's what Paul received from Ananias and from God. You and I can receive that same grace of God. Praise God for his generosity.*

> *Paul wrote:* This righteousness from God comes through faith in Jesus Christ to all who believe. There is no difference, for all have sinned and fall short of the glory of God, and are justified freely by his grace through the redemption that came by Christ Jesus. (Romans 3:22–24)

Follow the leader

Prepare *Sometimes church leaders appear in the news for the worst possible reasons. Any failure by someone who's supposed to be a moral guide makes very good tabloid reading. But being a church leader is a tough job, and they are just as human as we are. Thank God for the church leaders that you know and ask him to show you how you can encourage them.*

Read **Acts 15:5—8,10,11,13—15,19,20**

Paul and his right-hand man, Barnabas, reported how non-Jews had been turning to Jesus. [5] Then some of the believers who belonged to the party of the Pharisees stood up and said, "The Gentiles must be circumcised and required to obey the law of Moses." [6] The apostles and elders met to consider this question. [7] After much discussion, Peter got up and addressed them: "Brothers, you know that some time ago God made a choice among you that the Gentiles might hear from my lips the message of the gospel and believe. [8] God, who knows the heart, showed that he accepted them by giving the Holy Spirit to them, just as he did to us. [10] Now then, why do you try to test God by putting on the necks of the disciples a yoke that neither we nor our fathers have been able to bear? [11] No! We believe it is through the grace of our Lord Jesus that we are saved, just as they are." [13] When they finished, James spoke up: "Brothers, listen to me. [14] Simon has described to us how God at first showed his concern by taking from the Gentiles a people for himself. [15] The words of the prophets are in agreement with this. [19] It is my judgement, therefore, that we should not make it difficult for the Gentiles who are turning to God. [20] Instead we should write to them, telling them to abstain from food polluted by idols, from sexual immorality, from the meat of strangled animals and from blood."

Explore The early church faced a thorny issue: do people have to become Jews before they become Christians (v 5)? This makes sense considering that Jesus was the fulfilment of promises to the Jews, all the first Christians were Jews and they originally met in the Jewish places of worship. So the Christian leaders, basically the apostles, met in Jerusalem for a council. Peter argued persuasively that God had given his seal of approval to the Gentiles (non-Jews) by giving them the Holy Spirit (v 8), and the Jews had not been successful anyway in fulfilling the requirements of the sacrificial law (v 10). Both Gentiles and Jews are saved, not by observing any rituals, but by the free gift of God received through faith (v 11).

The council's decision is that only basic requirements will be placed on the Gentile converts. They should be sexually pure, and avoid eating foods that would stop Jewish believers and Gentile believers sitting down to a meal together (v 20). This process is as interesting as its outcome. The leadership discovers a grey area which has been causing conflict among believers, so they search the Scriptures and pray, and talk through the issue in a godly and wise manner. Just as the early believers obeyed the edict from Jerusalem, we need to take seriously the advice and warnings of our church leaders. Many churches today have a similar kind of council of elders, and they need our prayerful support.

Respond *Pray for church leaders, that they may be godly and wise.*

> *Peter described a good church leader:* Be shepherds of God's flock
> that is under your care, serving as overseers – not because you
> must, but because you are willing, as God wants you to be; not
> greedy for money, but eager to serve; not lording it over those
> entrusted to you, but being examples to the flock. (1 Peter 5:2,3)

day 40

Earth shattering

Prepare *Following Jesus is the kind of thing that will shake your life to its foundations. Are you ready for that? This is the last reading in our book. If you're willing, ask God to show you something today that will stay with you throughout your life.*

Read **Acts 16:25—34**

In the city of Philippi, Paul and Silas cast a spirit out of a slave girl who'd earned money for her owners by telling fortunes. In the ruckus that followed, they were flogged and thrown in jail. 25 About midnight Paul and Silas were praying and singing hymns to God, and the other prisoners were listening to them. 26 Suddenly there was such a violent earthquake that the foundations of the prison were shaken. At once all the prison doors flew open, and everybody's chains came loose. 27 The jailer woke up, and when he saw the prison doors open, he drew his sword and was about to kill himself because he thought the prisoners had escaped. 28 But Paul shouted, "Don't harm yourself! We are all here!" 29 The jailer called for lights, rushed in and fell trembling before Paul and Silas. 30 He then brought them out and asked, "Sirs, what must I do to be saved?" 31 They replied, "Believe in the Lord Jesus, and you will be saved – you and your household." 32 Then they spoke the word of the Lord to him and to all the others in his house. 33 At that hour of the night the jailer took them and washed their wounds; then immediately he and all his family were baptised. 34 The jailer brought them into his house and set a meal before them; he was filled with joy because he had come to believe in God – he and his whole family.

Explore Sceptics would say this earthquake was a coincidence, but as an African bishop once said, 'When I pray, coincidences happen.' Judging by the jailer's reaction (v 30), it was crystal clear to him that the spiritual noises he'd been hearing (v 25) were directly linked with the movement of the earth. Paul and Silas' refusal to dodge the legal ramifications of what they'd been doing (v 28) also made an impression. A seismic event occurred that night in the jailer's own life and that of all his family (v 33).

Not everybody becomes a Christian the instant they hear about Jesus. For some it is a slow process of inquiry and evaluation, but there comes a moment when we just have to acknowledge that we want to be saved, and Jesus is the answer.

Respond *If you've been weighing everything up as you've read this book, but you now find the evidence for Christianity compelling, don't sit on the fence any longer. Seize hold of Jesus and the rescue he offers you, believe in him and be baptised. If you're still uncertain, keep on asking questions, going to a church and seriously seeking the God of the universe – don't let anything deter you from your quest. If you already belong to Jesus, keep on getting to know him better, but also be brave in taking the message of Jesus to your friends and your household. Like the jailer in today's story, you've discovered overwhelming joy. Tell the people you love.*

> *Jesus said:* 'My sheep listen to my voice; I know them, and they follow me. I give them eternal life, and they shall never perish; no one can snatch them out of my hand. My Father, who has given them to me, is greater than all; no one can snatch them out of my Father's hand. I and the Father are one.' (John 10:27–30)

Where to now?

If you have chosen to follow Jesus, you are now part of a family with everyone else from every part of our planet who has made the same decision – God's family

I am sitting in my home in Brisbane, Australia, as I write this, looking out on a brilliant blue sky and my neighbour's lush tree ferns. You might be looking out on snowy mountains or busy city streets or vast plains or a sun-baked desert. We might have different passports and spend different currencies, and speak different dialects of the English language. But we are all one family. I love to travel, and I continually discover that I can meet someone for the first time, who is from a totally different background and culture to me, and we have an instant bond. I have friends who do not share my faith, and they are dear to me, but this special sense of connection is unique to my friendships with Christians.

Develop your family relationship by spending time with other family members. It is important to become part of a church fellowship, both for the support and encouragement they will give you, and for the support and encouragement you can give them.

Develop your relationship with your heavenly Father by spending time with him. Make a habit of prayer, both talking and listening. You won't always know what to say and how to say it. But it will gradually become more natural for you to talk to him about all sorts of things.

Keep on reading the Bible, God's major form of communication with you. Lots of Christians find it helps anchor them if they spend a little time reading each day. *Closer to God* produces a new guide every three months that you can use to help you read and understand God's message to you in the Bible. Ask a Christian book shop if you would like to continue with *Closer to God* or use the subscription form inside the back cover.

You have come to the end of the book, but, if you have become a Christian, it is only the beginning of a new life for you, filled with meaning and purpose, lived in intimate relationship with Jesus. Enjoy the adventure!

About Closer to God

It's amazing but true that reading the Bible regularly and expecting God, by his Holy Spirit, to speak through it can empower us all to live more like Jesus and to do the things he did. And *Closer to God* is written and put together by a team whose heart's desire is to help make that happen in your life.

Closer to God is for anyone who longs to hear God's voice in today's noisy world. If you believe or hope that God speaks to ordinary people; loving, freeing, changing and healing them, then *Closer to God* is for you.

Each issue contains three months of material and variety is key. For every week you'll find:

A scene-setting introduction.

Five main Bible readings with comments. Usually these form part of a comprehensive exploration of the Bible, but each issue also carries several theme weeks. A 'Bible in a year' plan at the foot of each note can be started at any time.

A meditation called Going deeper – a more experiential approach to a Bible theme raised during the week.

Looking outwards – a practical challenge for how to live out the Bible truths you've been examining in the real world.

Two extra readings with brief comments. If you read the Bible every day these will fit into Saturday and Sunday, but if you don't have time to include these the overall sense of the week's readings won't be affected.

There's also a magazine section called **UPclose**, with a range of features on living for Jesus, as well as interviews with high-profile Christians. In addition, each issue contains a colour bookmark – yours to tear out and use to mark your place.

Visit our interactive website at **www.closertogod.org.uk**

closer to
GOD

get
to
know

this man better...